Grammar & Usage
for Better Writing

AMSCO

AMSCO SCHOOL PUBLICATIONS, INC.

315 Hudson Street, New York, N.Y. 10013

Contributing Editors

Auditi Chakravarty
Director of Language Arts
Amsco School Publications, Inc.

Bonnie Boehme
Editor
Nesbitt Graphics, Inc.

This book has been adapted from the following Amsco publications:

Building Power in Writing
By Henry I. Christ

English Alive: Complete Edition
By Harold Levine

Text and cover design: Nesbitt Graphics, Inc.
Composition: Nesbitt Graphics, Inc.

When ordering this book please specify:
Either R 798 W *or* **GRAMMAR AND USAGE FOR BETTER WRITING**

Please visit our Web site at **www.amscopub.com**

ISBN 1-56765-117-8

NYC Item 56765-117-7

Printed in the United States of America.

1 2 3 4 6 7 8 9   08 07 06 05 04

Contents

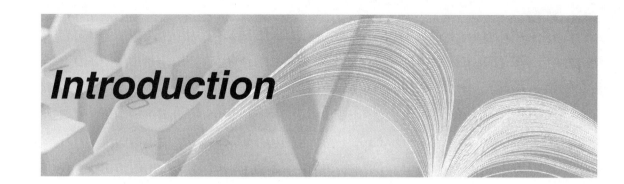

Introduction

How To Use This Book

Grammar and Usage for Better Writing is a basic workbook that can provide a foundation for further study in English grammar and usage. It will benefit students who are learning the essentials for the first time as well as those who wish to review concepts they have previously learned. The premise of this book is that understanding how language works enables us to use it more effectively. This skill can enhance our personal communications, schoolwork, and professional lives.

The workbook is organized into four major parts. The parts in turn consist of brief lessons, each with explanations, examples, and practice to ensure that students understand the concepts being introduced. The book is structured sequentially, with the most basic elements—the parts of a sentence—introduced in Part One, followed by the composition of sentences in Part Two. Part Three focuses on some common problems that people encounter when using English, and it places more emphasis on *applying* the rules. Students who are new to grammar study should begin with Part One and work through each section in order; more advanced students who already know the parts of speech may want to start with Part Two and use the first section for reference.

Once writers learn the parts of sentences and how they work together to determine the meaning and effect of a sentence, they can begin to understand what good writing is all about. Part Four is designed to help students make the transition from crafting sentences to developing good paragraphs, the foundation for most kinds of writing. It serves as an introduction to further study of rhetoric and composition.

Study the rules, review the examples, and look for more examples of good writing in books, newspapers, magazines, Web sites, and other available sources. Complete the exercises to practice what you have learned, but also remember to apply the rules whenever you speak and write. The more you use what you learn in this book, the better and more natural your use of the English language will be. In the end, you will be a stronger, more effective speaker and writer. You're on your way—good luck!

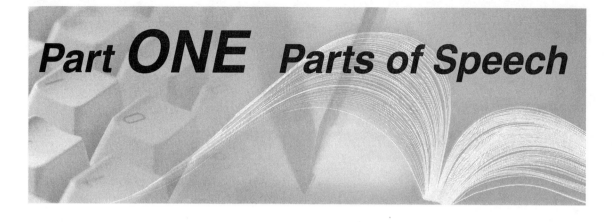

Part ONE Parts of Speech

In a sentence, a word may play one of eight parts. It may be either

1. a noun,
2. a pronoun,
3. a verb,
4. an adjective,

5. an adverb,
6. a preposition,
7. a conjunction, or
8. an interjection.

 These eight parts are known as the *parts of speech*.

We use the parts of speech to build sentences. For example, if we put together the noun *sunburn* and the verb *itches,* we can make the following statement:

Sunburn itches.
N.   V.

We can expand this statement by adding the adjective *my:*

My sunburn itches.
ADJ.   N.   V.

We can also add the adverb *painfully:*

My sunburn itches ***painfully.***
ADJ. N.   V.   ADV.

If we should want to ask a question, we can begin with a verb. Here is a question made up of the verb *is,* the noun *sunburn,* and the adjective *painful.*

Is sunburn painful?
V.   N.   ADJ.

Of course, we can expand this question. For example, we can add the adverb *usually*.

Is sunburn ***usually*** painful?
V.   N.   ADV.   ADJ.

The system that our language uses to put parts of speech together into sentences is known as *grammar*.

The first two lessons focus on the two basic parts of any sentence: the subject and the predicate.

Lesson 1 The Subject

A sentence has two parts: (1) a *subject* and (2) a *predicate*. This lesson deals with the subject.

> **The *subject* is the part of the sentence about which something is told or asked.**

The seats on the bus are very comfortable.

> QUESTION: About what is the sentence telling something?
>
> ANSWER: *The seats on the bus.*
>
> SUBJECT: *The seats on the bus.*

Amelia Earhart disappeared over the Pacific.

> QUESTION: About whom is the sentence telling something?
>
> ANSWER: *Amelia Earhart.*
>
> SUBJECT: *Amelia Earhart.*

Has your brother Tom found a summer job?

> QUESTION: About whom is the sentence asking something?
>
> ANSWER: *your brother Tom.*
>
> SUBJECT: *your brother Tom.*

Position of the Subject

The subject is usually found at the beginning of the sentence, but it can also appear in other positions.

SUBJECT AT THE BEGINNING OF THE SENTENCE:

> **<u>An experienced pilot</u> was at the controls at the time of the crash.**

SUBJECT AT THE END OF THE SENTENCE:

> **At the controls at the time of the crash was <u>an experienced pilot</u>.**

At the time of the crash, <u>an experienced pilot</u> was at the controls.

Finding the Subject

A sure way to find the subject is to answer one or the other of these questions:

- About whom or about what is the sentence saying or asking something?
- Who or what is doing, or has done, or will do something?

Question 1:	What is the subject of the following sentence? **The score at the end of the quarter was 12–12.**
Procedure:	Ask yourself: "About what is the sentence saying something?" Obviously, <u>The score at the end of the quarter</u>.
Answer:	The subject is <u>The score at the end of the quarter</u>. (The subject tells *about what* the sentence is saying something.)
Question 2:	What is the subject of the following sentence? **The orchestra members tuned their instruments.**
Procedure:	Ask yourself: "Who did something?"
Answer:	The subject is <u>The orchestra members</u>. (The subject tells *who* did something.)
Question 3:	What is the subject of the following? **Wait outside, please.**
Procedure:	Ask yourself: "Who is to wait outside?"
Answer:	The subject is <u>You</u> (understood). **(You) wait outside, please.**
Note:	In an imperative sentence (a sentence expressing a command or making a request), the subject *You* is not expressed but understood.
Question 4:	What is the subject of the following? **Is the door to the basement locked?**
Procedure:	Ask yourself: "Is what locked?"
Answer:	The subject is <u>the door to the basement</u>. (The subject tells *about what* the sentence is asking something.)

EXERCISE 1.   Write the subject in the space provided.

Sample:

The apples in the fruit bowl were all sour.

   The apples in the fruit bowl
_____

1. Next to the hardware store is a ski shop.

_____

2. Will your father drive us to the game?

_____

3. Is the noise from the next room bothering you?

_____

4. Our math teacher coaches the bowling team.

_____

5. The bowling team is coached by our math teacher.

_____

Simple Subject and Complete Subject

 When a subject consists of more than one word, the main word in that subject is called the *simple subject*.

The **seats** on the bus are very comfortable.
>   SIMPLE SUBJECT: seats

 The simple subject and the words that describe it are together known as the *complete subject*.

>   COMPLETE SUBJECT: The seats on the bus

Question: Does a simple subject ever consist of more than one word?

Answer: Yes, especially if it is a name. For example:

The late **Amelia Earhart** was a pioneer in aviation.
>   COMPLETE SUBJECT: The late Amelia Earhart
>   SIMPLE SUBJECT: Amelia Earhart

Sample:

The first reporters on the scene did not get all the facts.

C.S.   *The first reporters on the scene*   S.S.   *reporters*

Hint: You can be sure that you have correctly chosen the simple subject if you can prove to yourself that it cannot be omitted. If *The, first,* and *on the scene* were omitted from the C.S., above, the sentence would still make sense. But if *reporters* were omitted, the sentence would not make sense. This proves that *reporters* is the simple subject.

1. The famous *Mona Lisa* is a painting by Leonardo da Vinci.

   C.S. _____   S.S. _____

2. Did a letter from your sister come this morning?

   C.S. _____   S.S. _____

3. Farther up on the hill is a house with white shutters.

   C.S. _____   S.S. _____

4. Asleep in the crib was a six-month-old baby.

   C.S. _____   S.S. _____

5. My older brother is graduating in June.

   C.S. _____   S.S. _____

Lesson 2 The Predicate

Before we talk about the *predicate,* remember that

 The *subject* is the part of the sentence about which something is told or asked.

<u>Prices</u> are higher.
subject

What Is the Predicate?

 The *predicate* is the part of the sentence that tells or asks something about the subject.

Prices <u><u>are higher</u></u> .
predicate

You can easily find the subject and the predicate of a sentence by asking two simple questions:

Prices are higher.

QUESTION 1: About what is the sentence telling something?

ANSWER: *Prices.*

The subject is <u>*Prices*</u>.

QUESTION 2: What is the sentence saying about *Prices?*

ANSWER: Prices *are higher.*

The predicate is <u>*are higher*</u>.

My sister Karen is waiting for us.

QUESTION 1: About whom is the sentence telling something?

ANSWER: *My sister Karen.*

The subject is <u>*My sister Karen*</u>.

QUESTION 2:   What is the sentence saying about *My sister Karen?*

ANSWER: My sister Karen *is waiting for us.*

The predicate is *is waiting for us.*

Was Andy angry?

QUESTION 1:   About whom is the sentence asking something?

ANSWER: *Andy.*

The subject is *Andy.*

QUESTION 2:   What is the sentence asking about *Andy?*

ANSWER: *Was* Andy *angry?*

The predicate is *Was angry.*

Position of the Predicate

The predicate usually comes after the subject, but it can also appear in other positions.

PREDICATE AFTER THE SUBJECT:

The parking lot is next to the stadium.
S.   P.

PREDICATE BEFORE THE SUBJECT:

Next to the stadium is the parking lot.
P.   S.

PREDICATE PARTLY BEFORE AND PARTLY AFTER THE SUBJECT:

Is the parking lot next to the stadium?
P.   S.   P.

EXERCISE 1.   First draw a single line under the complete subject of the sentence. Then, above the double line at the right, write the predicate.

Samples:

SUBJECT	PREDICATE
The temperature dropped suddenly.	*dropped suddenly*
Has the plane landed?	*Has . . . landed*
Under the tree lay many rotting apples.	*Under the tree lay*

1. Has our teacher recovered from the flu? _____

2. Behind the wheel was my sister Maria. _____

3. How comfortable these new seats are! _____

4. Finally, the suspect surrendered to the police. _____

5. A flock of seagulls landed on the beach. _____

EXERCISE 2.   Complete the sentence by adding a predicate.

Samples:

The apple   *was not ripe.* _____

A speck of dust   *flew into my eye.* _____

1. The onion soup _____

2. Your suede jacket _____

3. Her new pen _____

4. The owner of the car _____

5. My desk at home _____

Lesson 3 Verbs

 The main word in the predicate is called the *verb*.

Here are a few examples:

1. The temperature ***dropped*** rapidly.

    PREDICATE: dropped rapidly

    VERB: dropped

2. José often ***visits*** exhibits at the natural history museum.

    PREDICATE: often visits exhibits at the natural history museum

    VERB: visits

3. ***Have*** you no sense?

    PREDICATE: Have no sense

    VERB: Have

Without a verb, the predicate cannot tell or ask anything about the subject. For instance, if the verb *dropped* is left out of the first sentence above, the resulting sentence cannot convey any clear meaning:

The temperature. . . rapidly.

Question: Does a verb ever consist of more than one word?

Answer: Yes, often. A verb may consist of one to four words:

SENTENCE	VERB
They have no questions.	have
Do you have any questions?	Do . . . have
We have been calling John all week.	have been calling
His phone may have been disconnected.	may have been disconnected

EXERCISE 1.   Find the verb and write it in the blank space.

Samples:

Ben was at the door.   *was*

They must have been treated badly.   *must have been treated*

1. Mindy has a lot of friends.   _____

2. The water is boiling in the microwave.   _____

3. I should have listened to you.   _____

4. He must have been pushed by someone
   in the crowd.   _____

5. Did the light bother you?   _____

EXERCISE 2.   Write the *simple subject* in the **S.S.** space, the *predicate* in the **P.** space, and the *verb* in the **V.** space.

Samples:

The pond froze during the night.   S.S. __*pond*_____

                                                              P.   __*froze during the night*_____

                                                              V.   __*froze*_____

Wash your hands.   S.S. __*You* (understood)_____

                                                              P.   __*Wash your hands*_____

                                                              V.   __*Wash*_____

Did you hear the wind?   S.S. __*You*_____

                                                              P.   __*Did hear the wind*_____

                                                              V.   __*Did hear*_____

1. Comb your hair.   S.S. _____

                                                              P.   _____

                                                              V.   _____

2. The bus will come at any minute.   S.S. _____

                                                              P.   _____

                                                              _____

                                                              V.   _____

3. Has it been coming on time lately?

S.S. _____

P. _____

_____

V. _____

4. For some time, light rain has been falling.

S.S. _____

P. _____

_____

V. _____

5. It must have been raining since dawn.

S.S. _____

P. _____

_____

V. _____

6. In my pocket was the missing glove.

S.S. _____

P. _____

_____

V. _____

7. Fuel bills have been increasing every year.

S.S. _____

P. _____

_____

V. _____

8. The cold weather has been affecting the spring crops.

S.S. _____

P. _____

_____

V. _____

9. Does your remote control need fresh batteries?

S.S. _____

P. _____

_____

V. _____

10. Someone must have taken my books by mistake.

S.S. _____

P. _____

_____

V. _____

Action and Linking Verbs

ACTION VERBS

What Is an Action Verb?

An *action verb* is a verb that expresses action.

There are two kinds of action verbs:

1. Verbs that express *physical action*—action that can be seen or *heard*:

   The car ***skidded, left*** the road, and ***smashed*** into a telephone pole.
   (*Skidded, left,* and *smashed* express physical action.)

2. Verbs that express *mental action*—action that takes place in the mind and therefore cannot be seen or heard:

   We ***believed*** and ***trusted*** them because we ***knew*** them.
   (*Believed, trusted,* and *knew* express mental action.)

EXERCISE 1.   If the italicized verb expresses physical action, write **P** in the space provided. If it expresses mental action, write **M.**

Samples:

Pat *tagged* the runner.	*P*
Did you *understand* the lesson?	*M*

1. I *forgot* the combination.   _____

2. *Open* a window.   _____

3. Who *rang* the bell?   _____

4. He *considers* me his best friend.   _____

5. We *are hoping* for the best this season.   _____

LINKING VERBS

Not all verbs are action verbs. The verb *is* in the following sentence does not express action. It is a *linking verb.*

Jordan *is* angry at us.
L.V.

What Is a Linking Verb?

In the preceding sentence, the verb *is* has little meaning of its own. Its main function is to *link* (connect) *Jordan* with *angry*. For this reason, we call *is* a *linking verb*.

 A *linking verb* links (connects) the subject with a word in the predicate that describes or identifies the subject.

The road *was* slippery.
L.V.

(*Slippery* describes the subject *road*.)

Ama *is* the captain of the volleyball team.
L.V.

(*Captain* identifies the subject *Ama*.)

What Are Some Common Linking Verbs?

1. The most frequently used linking verb is *be*, whose forms include the following:

   am, are, is, was, were.

   Of course, verb phrases ending in *be*, *being*, and *been* are also linking verbs:

   will be, would be, are being, have been, could have been, etc.

2. In addition, each of the following verbs can be either an action verb or a linking verb, depending on the way it is used.

VERB	USED AS ACTION VERB	USED AS LINKING VERB
appear	The principal *appeared* at 10 a.m.	Fred *appeared* tired.
become	The haircut *becomes* (suits) her.	My room *becomes* messy.
feel	Did you *feel* the cloth?	I *feel* nervous.
grow	Farmers *grow* crops.	The days *grow* longer.
look	We *looked* the place over.	He *looked* unhappy.
smell	I *smelled* smoke.	The air *smelled* salty.
sound	Who *sounded* the alarm?	Her voice *sounded* hoarse.

taste	I *tasted* the soup.	The soup *tasted* delicious.
turn	She *turned* the page.	The weather *turned* cold.

How Can a Linking Verb Be Recognized?

If a verb can be replaced with some form of the verb *be,* it is a linking verb.

Question 1:   Is *feels* a linking verb in the following sentence?
Jordan *feels* angry.

Answer: We can replace *feels* with *is* (a form of the verb *be*).
Jordan *is* angry.
Therefore, *feels,* in the above sentence, is a linking verb.

Question 2:   Is *feels* a linking verb in the following sentence?
The patient *feels* pain.

Answer: In this sentence, we cannot replace *feels* with *is.*
Therefore, *feels* here is not a linking verb. It is an action verb.

Summary: **An *action verb* expresses action, either physical or mental.**

A *linking verb* connects the subject with a word in the predicate that describes or identifies the subject.

EXERCISE 2.   Is the verb in the sentence an action verb or a linking verb? Write your answer in the space provided.

Samples:

Nancy *broke* her arm.	*action*
Joe *looks* tired.	*linking*

1. Today, I *feel* better. _____

2. This blouse *looks* new. _____

3. I *smelled* the fish. _____

4. Mei *tasted* the melon. _____

5. Her cookies *tasted* delicious. _____

6. Your voice *sounded* hoarse. _____

7. She *looked* through the whole book. _____

8. We *were* exhausted. _____

9. Courtney *looked* amazed by the whole event. _____

10. Did you *feel* the energy in that room? _____

Helping Verbs and Verb Phrases

What Is a Helping Verb?

Sometimes a verb consists of more than one word:

> The letters ***have been mailed.***
>   verb

In *have been mailed, mailed* is the **main verb;** *have* and *been* are ***helping verbs.***

> The letters ***have been mailed.***
>   H.V.   H.V.   M.V.

 Helping verbs are verbs that come before and "help" the main verb.

A main verb may have as many as three helping verbs.

| ONE HELPING VERB: | Anne ***has*** mailed the letters. |
| | H.V.   M.V. |

| TWO HELPING VERBS: | The letters ***have been*** mailed. |
| | H.V. H.V.   M.V. |

| THREE HELPING VERBS: | They ***should have been*** mailed earlier. |
| | H.V. H.V. H.V.   M.V. |

What Is a Verb Phrase?

 When a verb consists of one or more helping verbs plus a main verb, it is called a *verb phrase*.

HELPING VERB(S)	+ MAIN VERB	= VERB PHRASE
has	+ mailed	= has mailed
have been	+ mailed	= have been mailed
should have been	+ mailed	= should have been mailed

Which Verbs Can Be Used as Helping Verbs?

Below is a list of verbs commonly used as helping verbs (note that *be,* which we studied earlier as a linking verb, page 14, can also be a helping verb):

be, am, are, is, was, were, being, been	can, could
have, has, had	will, would
do, does, did	shall, should
may, might	must

EXERCISE 1. Indicate the *verb phrase, helping verb* or *verbs*, and *main verb* in each of the following sentences.

Sample:

Leaves have been falling all week.
V. PHR.   *have been falling*
H.V.   *have been*
M.V.   *falling*

1. The Eagles could have protested the decision.
V. PHR.
H.V.
M.V.

2. You should have seen the mess!
V. PHR.
H.V.
M.V.

3. I must have left my wallet at home.
V. PHR.
H.V.
M.V.

4. Justin has been acting strange lately.
V. PHR.
H.V.
M.V.

5. They have played basketball for two seasons.

    V. PHR. _____

    H.V. _____

    M.V. _____

Word Order in Questions

In questions, we usually put the subject after the first helping verb.

Are tickets being collected?
H.V.   S.

(The subject *tickets* comes after the first helping verb *Are*.)

EXERCISE 2.   Change the following statements to questions.

Sample:

The tire has been repaired.   *Has the tire been repaired?* _____

1. The argument has been settled.   _____

2. Lauren will buy the refreshments.   _____

3. It has been pouring rain all day.   _____

4. We should have waited a bit longer.   _____

5. Our team could have done better.   _____

Reminder: Did you end each of your questions above with a question mark?

Composition Hint

Shorten your verb phrases whenever possible. Avoid *wordiness*—the use of unnecessary words. Aim for *conciseness*—brief, uncluttered expression.

WORDY: If you do not run for president, she **_may run_**.

CONCISE: If you do not run for president, she **_may_**.
          (The main verb *run* is understood.)

WORDY: Jim refused to apologize. He **_should have apologized_**.

CONCISE: Jim refused to apologize. He **_should have_**.
          (The main verb *apologized* is understood.)

WORDY: They are not being blamed, but I *am being blamed.*

CONCISE: They are not being blamed, but I *am.*
            (The helping verb *being* and the main verb *blamed* are understood.)

EXERCISE 3.   Make each of the following sentences more concise by shortening a verb phrase.

Sample:

I could have waited, and perhaps I should have waited.

I could have waited, and perhaps I should have.

1. She does not have to go, but I have to go.

_____

2. They were supposed to be paid; they were not paid.

_____

3. If Sharon does not complain, no one else will complain.

_____

4. My word is being questioned, but your word is not being questioned.

_____

5. We did not quit, though we should have quit.

_____

Verbs in Contractions

 A *contraction* is a combination of two words with one or more letters omitted.

Suppose a friend asks whether you would rather eat lunch at twelve or one. The time does not matter to you.
What would you say to your friend?

   1. It does not matter.

   2. It doesn't matter.

You would probably say:

It doesn't matter.

In informal conversation, we tend to use contractions. For example, we combine *does* with *not,* forming the contraction *doesn't.*

Note that *not,* the second word in the contraction, loses the letter *o,* and in place of that *o* we have an apostrophe: **doesn't.**

In contractions consisting of a verb plus *not, not* loses an *o.*

VERB	+ NOT	= CONTRACTION	LETTER(S) OMITTED
is	+ not	= *isn't*	*o*
are	+ not	= *aren't*	*o*
would	+ not	= *wouldn't*	*o*

In one case, *not* loses an *n* and an *o:*

can	+ not	= *can't*	*n o*

Finally, learn this irregular (unusual) contraction:

will	+ not	= *won't*

EXERCISE 1.   Write the contraction.

Sample:

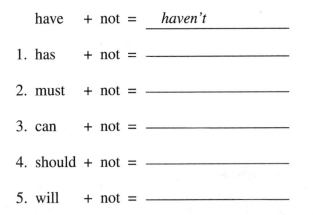

have   + not =   *haven't*   _____

1. has   + not = _____

2. must   + not = _____

3. can   + not = _____

4. should + not = _____

5. will   + not = _____

Contractions are entirely natural and correct in *informal* English (friendly notes, everyday conversation). However, they are not ordinarily used in *formal* English (business letters, letters of application, term papers, reports).

EXERCISE 2.   Change each of the following contractions to *formal* English.

Samples:

didn't	*did not*
I've	*I have*

1. hasn't _____   6. can't _____

2. isn't _____   7. weren't _____

3. won't _____   8. you'd _____

4. I'll _____   9. wasn't _____

5. shouldn't _____   10. it's _____

The contraction *ain't* is considered nonstandard. This means that *ain't* should not be used in either formal or informal English situations. Avoid it.

INSTEAD OF	USE
I *ain't* ready.	**I'm not ready.**
	or **I am not ready.**
Ain't I next?	**Am I not next?**
They *ain't* come back.	**They haven't come back.**
	or **They have not come back.**

Lesson 4 Nouns

 Nouns **are words that name persons, animals, places, or things.**

Question 1:   How many nouns are there in the following sentence?

An old fisherman who had no luck hooked a huge fish that pulled his boat far out to sea.

Answer: Five.
1. fisherman (a person)
2. luck (a thing)
3. fish (an animal)
4. boat (a thing)
5. sea (a place)

Nouns name things we can see and touch, like *boat,* as well as things we cannot see or touch, like *luck.*

Question 2:   How many nouns does the following sentence contain?

Divers fish for pearls in the Gulf of Mexico.

Answer: Three.
1. Divers (persons)
2. pearls (things)
3. Gulf of Mexico (a place)

Note that *fish,* which was a noun in the earlier sentence, is not one here because *it does not name anything.* Here, *fish* is a *verb* (a word that expresses action).

Question 3:   May a noun consist of more than one word?

Answer: Yes. *Gulf of Mexico* is one noun. **Nouns of more than one word are called *compound nouns*.** Here are more examples of compound nouns:

living room
Atlantic Ocean
Grand Central Parkway
Mr. Applebaum
sister-in-law

EXERCISE 1. Look at the italicized word. If it is used as a noun, write **N.** in the space provided. If it is used as a verb, write **V.**

Sample:

    a. We always *lock* the door.   *V.*

    b. Can you open the *lock*?   *N.*

1. *a.* I ate three *slices* of pizza.   _____

    b. This machine *slices* bread.   _____

2. *a.* Many birds *fly* south for the winter.   _____

    b. A *fly* buzzed past my ear.   _____

3. *a.* You have a great *smile*.   _____

    b. *Smile* for the camera.   _____

4. *a.* Oatmeal *cooks* in a few minutes.   _____

    b. Good *cooks* make delicious meals.   _____

5. *a.* Please *hand* me that book.   _____

    b. Your *hand* is bleeding.   _____

EXERCISE 2. List all the nouns in the following sentences.

Samples:

The driver stopped at the post office to mail a package.

   driver, post office, package

My soul has grown deep like the rivers. (Langston Hughes)

   soul, rivers

1. Fog forced the airport to close.

2. The fleet has left the Indian Ocean.

3. Mrs. Thorpe has invited two sisters and a brother-in-law to her son's graduation.

---

4. Mr. Jones of the Manor Farm had locked the hen-houses for the night, but was too drunk to remember to shut the popholes. (George Orwell)

_____

5. In March, the weather is unsettled, blackbirds return, and trees begin to send out new leaves.

_____

6. Jamie was in the driveway washing her car with a hose and a few sponges.

_____

7. George went back through the swinging-door into the kitchen and untied Nick and the cook. (Ernest Hemingway)

_____

8. New York City has a larger population than San Francisco.

_____

9. Have some more beans and rice.

_____

10. Did the team show any signs of improvement in the second quarter?

_____

Common and Proper Nouns

Compare the following sentences:

1. We are approaching a lake.
2. We are approaching Lake Michigan.

In sentence 1, we call _lake_ a _common noun_. In sentence 2, we call _Lake Michigan_ a _proper noun_.

What Is a Proper Noun?

 A _proper noun_ refers to _one particular person, animal, place, or thing_—like _Lake Michigan_ in sentence 2.

A proper noun is _always capitalized_.

What Is a Common Noun?

 A *common noun* refers to *no particular person, animal, place, or thing*, but to any one at all—like *lake* in sentence 1.

A common noun is *not* capitalized.

Here are some more examples of common and proper nouns.

COMMON NOUNS (*not* capitalized)	PROPER NOUNS (*always* capitalized)
day (any day)	Monday
month (any month)	April
bridge (any bridge)	Golden Gate Bridge
ocean (any ocean)	Pacific Ocean
event (any event)	Olympics
magazine (any magazine)	*Newsweek*
institution (any institution)	Congress
language (any language)	Spanish
boy (any boy)	Jim
girl (any girl)	Brittany

EXERCISE 1.   List the common and proper nouns in the following sentences.

Sample:

Bourbon Street is a lively street in New Orleans.

The Brooklyn Bridge is the oldest bridge over the East River.

COMMON NOUNS: *street*

PROPER NOUNS: *Bourbon Street, New Orleans*

1. George Washington and Abraham Lincoln were born in February.

   COMMON NOUNS: _____

   PROPER NOUNS: _____

2. Call Adam from the airport as soon as the plane lands in Dallas.

   COMMON NOUNS: _____

   PROPER NOUNS: _____

3. Traffic is heavy in both directions on Interstate 99 and the roads feeding into it.

   COMMON NOUNS: _____

   PROPER NOUNS: _____

4. Considerable attention has been given by the press to the pollution of our lakes and rivers.

   COMMON NOUNS: _____

   PROPER NOUNS: _____

5. Rice University and Baylor College of Medicine are both in Houston.

   COMMON NOUNS: _____

   PROPER NOUNS: _____

EXERCISE 2.   Rewrite each sentence, changing the italicized common noun to a proper noun.

Sample:

An *ocean* is a vast body of water.

   The Pacific Ocean *is a vast body of water.* _____

1. A *girl* was named captain.

   _____

2. We will meet outside the *restaurant*.

   _____

3. I saw an accident on the *street*.

   _____

4. Tomorrow is a *holiday*.

   _____

5. A *boy* asked a question.

   _____

6. When are you returning to the *city*?

   _____

7. My father was reading the *newspaper*.

   _____

8. Does the *park* have tennis courts?

_____

9. We are four miles from the *river*.

_____

10. I was talking to a *neighbor*.

_____

Plural Nouns

Nouns have a *singular* form and a *plural* form.

 The *singular* is the form that means *only one*:

boy, girl, soda, hamburger, etc.

 The *plural* is the form that means *more than one*:

boys, girls, sodas, hamburgers, etc.

EXERCISE 1.   Write the form indicated.

Samples:

the plural of *window*   *windows* _____

the singular of *kittens*   *kitten* _____

1. the singular of *chairs*   _____

2. the plural of *passenger*   _____

3. the singular of *gloves*   _____

4. the plural of *bandage*   _____

5. the plural of *tree*   _____

Here are the singular and plural forms of a few more nouns.

SINGULAR (only one)	PLURAL (more than one)
1. hat	hats
2. box	boxes
3. leaf	leaves
4. foot	feet

From the above examples, you can see that there is no single rule for forming the plural of nouns; there are several. If you memorize the rules and do the exercises carefully, you will be well on your way to spelling plurals correctly.

Rule 1. For most nouns:

Add *s* to the singular to form the plural.

SINGULAR	PLURAL
ear	+ <u>s</u> = ears
chair	+ <u>s</u> = chairs
table	+ <u>s</u> = tables
face	+ <u>s</u> = faces

Question: Can I form the plural of words like *class* or *dish* by just adding *s?*

Answer: No, because [class<u>s</u>] and [dish<u>s</u>] would be hard to pronounce. We must do something else. This brings us to Rule 2.

Rule 2. For nouns ending in *s, sh, ch,* or *x:*

Add *es* to form the plural.

NOUNS ENDING IN *s:*	class + <u>es</u> = classes
	dress + <u>es</u> = dresses
NOUNS ENDING IN *sh:*	dish + <u>es</u> = dishes
	wish + <u>es</u> = wishes
NOUNS ENDING IN *ch:*	bench + <u>es</u> = benches
	lunch + <u>es</u> = lunches
NOUNS ENDING IN *x:*	box + <u>es</u> = boxes
	tax + <u>es</u> = taxes

Exceptions: The following nouns add neither *s* nor *es,* but form their plurals in an irregular way:

man	men
woman	women
child	children

foot	feet
tooth	teeth
louse	lice
mouse	mice
goose	geese
ox	oxen

EXERCISE 2.   Write the plural of the following nouns.

Samples:

hand	*hands*
wish	*wishes*
foot	*feet*

1. apple _____   9. woman _____

2. price _____   10. annex _____

3. ox _____   11. eyelash _____

4. fee _____   12. mouse _____

5. wax _____   13. goose _____

6. child _____   14. radish _____

7. glass _____   15. genius _____

8. louse _____

EXERCISE 3.   Make the following nouns singular.

Sample:

grandchildren	*grandchild*

1. lamps _____

2. gentlemen _____

3. addresses _____

4. flowers _____

5. circuses _____

Rule 3. **For most nouns ending in *f:***

Add *s* to form the plural.

$$belief + \underline{s} = beliefs$$
$$grief + \underline{s} = griefs$$
$$roof + \underline{s} = roofs$$

Exceptions: The following nouns ending in *f* change *f* to *v* and add *es:*

leaf	leaves
loaf	loaves
half	halves
self	selves
shelf	shelves
thief	thieves
wolf	wolves

But not in a name:

Mr. Wolf   The Wolfs

Rule 4. **For three nouns ending in *fe—knife*, *life*, and *wife*:**

Change *f* to *v* and add *s* to form the plural.

knife	knives
life	lives
wife	wives

EXERCISE 4.   Write the plural of the following nouns.

1. thief   _____

2. riff   _____

3. loaf   _____

4. grief   _____

5. roof   _____

6. proof   _____

7. half   _____

8. cliff   _____

9. self   _____

10. elf   _____

EXERCISE 5.   Make the following nouns singular.

Sample:

    knives   *knife* _____

1. leaves   _____

2. staffs   _____

3. lives   _____

4. selves   _____

5. churches   _____

Plural of Nouns Ending in *y*

To form the plural of a noun ending in *y*—like *way* or *lady*—first ask:

Is the letter before *y* a *vowel* or a *consonant?*

Remember that the *vowels* are *a, e, i, o,* and *u.* All of the other letters of the alphabet are *consonants.*

Now follow Rule 5 or 6.

Rule 5.   If the letter before *y* is a *vowel,* add *s* to form the plural.

SINGULAR	PLURAL
way + <u>s</u> =	ways
key + <u>s</u> =	keys
toy + <u>s</u> =	toys

Rule 6.   If the letter before *y* is a *consonant,* change the *y* to *i* and add *es.*

SINGULAR	PLURAL
lady	lad<u>ies</u>
enemy	enem<u>ies</u>
spy	sp<u>ies</u>

NOUNS   **31**

Samples:

journey	*journeys*
factory	*factories*

1. valley _____

2. baby _____

3. party _____

4. highway _____

5. company _____

6. joy _____

7. bakery _____

8. monkey _____

9. pharmacy _____

10. chimney _____

EXERCISE 7. Make the following nouns singular.

Samples:

pennies	*penny*
turkeys	*turkey*

1. holidays _____

2. juries _____

3. attorneys _____

4. ferries _____

5. bluejays _____

Plural of Nouns Ending in *o*

Rule 7. **If a noun ends in a *vowel plus o*, add *s* to form the plural.**

ENDING	SINGULAR	PLURAL
VOWEL e + *o*	stereo + <u>s</u> =	stereos
VOWEL i + *o*	radio + <u>s</u> =	radios

Rule 8. **If a noun ends in a *consonant plus o*, add *s* in most cases.**

auto + <u>s</u> = autos

two + <u>s</u> = twos

alto + <u>s</u> = altos

piano + <u>s</u> = pianos

Exceptions: Add *es* to the following nouns:

potato + <u>es</u> = potatoes

tomato + <u>es</u> = tomatoes

echo + <u>es</u> = echoes

veto + <u>es</u> = vetoes

EXERCISE 8. Make the following nouns plural.

Sample:

patio   *patios*

1. studio   _____

2. rodeo   _____

3. potato   _____

4. portfolio   _____

5. tomato   _____

6. ratio   _____

7. veto   _____

8. trio   _____

9. echo _____

10. piano _____

Possessive Nouns

 A *possessive noun* is a noun that shows possession or ownership. A *possessive noun* always contains an *apostrophe* ['].

Here are some examples of possessive nouns:

1. *student's* money The possessive noun *student's* shows that the money belongs to the student.

2. *students'* money The possessive noun *students'* shows that the money belongs to the students.

3. *children's* money The possessive noun *children's* shows that the money belongs to the children.

Note that a possessive noun can help us express ourselves in fewer words. For example, we can say the *children's money* (two words) instead of the *money belonging to the children* (five words).

Question: Why does the apostrophe come before the *s* in examples 1 and 3, above, but after the *s* in example 2?

Answer: Over the centuries, English has developed three rules for using the apostrophe to show possession.

Rule 1.   **If the possessor is a SINGULAR NOUN, add an APOSTROPHE AND S.**

the eyes of the *baby*   becomes the **baby's** eyes

the whiskers of the *cat*   becomes the **cat's** whiskers

the novels by *Dickens*   becomes **Dickens's** novels

EXERCISE 1.   Express each of the following phrases in fewer words.

Sample:

the name of the visitor   *the visitor's name* _____

1. the bark of the dog   _____

2. the books belonging to Justin _____

3. the car that Jessica owns _____

4. the house where Joe lives _____

5. the letter Ian wrote _____

Rule 2. **If the possessor is a PLURAL NOUN ENDING IN *s*, add ONLY AN APOSTROPHE.**

the lab experiments performed by the *girls*   becomes the **girls'** lab experiments

the coats owned by the *students*   becomes the **students'** coats

the nests of *birds*   becomes the **birds'** nests

EXERCISE 2.   Express in fewer words.

1. the mailboxes of neighbors   _____

2. tools used by carpenters   _____

3. the uniforms nurses wear   _____

4. the reasons the senators gave   _____

5. the money belonging to the depositors   _____

Rule 3. **If the possessor is a PLURAL NOUN *NOT* ENDING IN *s*, first write the plural; then add an APOSTROPHE AND *s*.**

shoes worn by *men*   becomes **men's** shoes

suits for *women*   becomes **women's** suits

the faces of *people*   becomes **people's** faces

EXERCISE 3.   Express in fewer words.

1. the names of the grandchildren   _____

2. the luggage belonging to the Englishmen   _____

3. the salaries the men earned   _____

4. the protests of the townspeople   _____

5. the reasons given by the women   _____

EXERCISE 4.   Write the correct possessive form of the noun in parentheses.

Sample:

My   *brother's* _____ name is Jack. (*brother*)

1. I borrowed my _____ biology notes. (*friend*)

2. My _____ names are Lee, Emily, and Sarah. (*sisters*)

3. Where did you put _____ umbrella? (*Ellen*)

4. There is a sale on _____ slacks. (*women*)

5. A dictator has little regard for _____ wishes. (*people*)

6. The _____ names are Madame Vigny and
   Madame Strauss. (*Frenchwomen*)

7. Are you _____ sister? (*Dennis*)

8. I borrowed my _____ snow shovel. (*neighbor*)

9. Have the _____ passes been distributed? (*visitors*)

10. The British advance was slowed by the _____ resistance.
    (*Minutemen*)

Composition Hint

When you write a paragraph, or even a sentence, see if you can reduce the number of words you have used. Sometimes, a possessive noun can help. For example,

INSTEAD OF: the car that my brother has   (6 words),

WRITE: my **brother's** car   (3 words).
             possessive
             noun

EXERCISE 5.   Rewrite the following paragraph, using possessive nouns wherever
possible. You should be able to reduce the number of words in the paragraph from
69 to 56.

The dog that Anja owns is huge but gentle. He tries to get the attention of her friends to show that he likes them. The parents of Anja, too, are fond of the dog. At first some neighbors were frightened by the size of the dog. They feared for the safety of their children. Now they no longer worry. By the way, the name of the dog is Tiny.

_____

_____

_____

_____

_____

_____

Lesson 5 Compound Subjects

 A *compound subject* consists of two or more subjects of the same verb connected by *and* or *or*.

1. Erin **and** Sean joined our group.
   compound subject   verb

   > *Erin* is a subject of the verb *joined*.
   > *Sean* is also a subject of the verb *joined*.

These two subjects of the same verb, connected by *and*, give us the compound subject *Erin and Sean.*

2. Nickels, dimes, **or** quarters may be deposited.
   compound subject   verb

   > *Nickels* is a subject of the verb *may be deposited*.
   > So, too, are *dimes* and *quarters.*

These three subjects of the same verb, connected by *or*, give us the compound subject *Nickels, dimes, or quarters.*

Composition Hint _____

> Compound subjects let us express ourselves in fewer words and without repetition. If there were no compound subjects, we would have to say:
>
> > Nickels may be deposited. Dimes may be deposited.
> > Quarters may be deposited.

EXERCISE 1.   Enter the compound subject in the space at the right.

Samples:

Rain or snow is predicted.	*Rain or snow*
Did Terry and Mallika agree with you?	*Terry and Mallika*

1. Vermont and New Hampshire are next to each other. _____

2. Are onions, lettuce, and carrots on your
   shopping list?

_____

3. Paula, Emilio, or I will help with the
   decorations.

_____

4. Cycling and rollerblading are my favorite
   sports.

_____

5. Saturday and Sunday, fog and mist made
   travel difficult.

_____

EXERCISE 2.   Express the following in fewer words by using a compound subject.

Samples:

Your battery may be causing the trouble.	_Your battery or bulb may be_
Your bulb may be causing the trouble.	_causing the trouble._
Dresses are on sale.	_Dresses, sweaters, and jackets are_
Sweaters are on sale.	_on sale._
Jackets are on sale.	

Note: When there are more than two subjects in a compound subject, put a comma after
each one, except the last:

Dresses, slacks, and jackets . . .

1. The House passed the bill.

   The Senate passed the bill.

_____

2. Carmela may be the next class president.

   Razi may be the next class president.

_____

3. Prices have gone up.

   Wages have gone up.

   Taxes have gone up.

_____

4. A table will be needed.

   Four chairs will be needed.

_____

5. The classrooms should be repainted.

   The science labs should be repainted.

_____

6. Lisa will be there.

   Jennifer will be there.

   Marie will be there.

7. CDs are better than tapes.

   DVDs are better than tapes.

8. Marlo could have scored the winning run.

   Alex could have scored the winning run.

9. A sensible diet is good for us.

   Exercise is good for us.

10. Notebooks are in the backpack.

    Pens are in the backpack.

EXERCISE 3. Complete each sentence below by adding a compound subject.

Samples:

_____*Friday and Saturday*_____ are the busiest shopping days of the week.

Did _____*Jennifer or Rajani*_____ tell you about my accident?

1. _____ are the coldest months of the year.

2. _____ will probably be chosen captain.

3. In yesterday's game, _____ did most of the scoring.

4. _____ had birthdays recently.

5. _____ broadcast the latest weather reports.

Lesson 6 Compound Verbs

 A *compound verb* consists of two or more verbs of the same subject connected by *and*, *or*, or *but*.

The <u>runner</u> <u>stumbled **and** fell</u>.
　　S.　　　compound verb

The verb *stumbled* tells what the subject *runner* did.

The verb *fell,* too, tells what the subject *runner* did.

These two verbs of the same subject, connected by *and*, give us the compound verb *stumbled and fell.*

Here are more examples of compound verbs:

The <u>wind</u> <u>moaned, whistled, **and** howled</u> all night.
　　S.　　　　compound verb

At night <u>I</u> often <u>read **or** watch</u> television.
　　　　　S.　　　compound verb

The old <u>car</u> <u>runs **but** uses</u> a lot of oil.
　　　　S.　compound verb

Question: May a sentence have both a compound subject and a compound verb?

Answer: Yes. Here is an example:

<u>Cindy **and** Luke</u> <u>sang **and** danced.</u>
compound subject　　compound verb

Composition Hint _____

A common error in writing is unnecessary repetition of the subject.

I parked the car. *I* shut off the engine. *I* put the key in my pocket.　(Three *I*'s.)

With a compound verb, we can avoid such repetition.

I parked the car, shut off the engine, and put the key in my pocket.　(One *I*.)

EXERCISE 1.   Eliminate repetition of the subject by using a compound verb.

Samples:

She jogs.

She swims.

She plays tennis.

She jogs, swims, and plays

tennis.

We tried.

We did not succeed.

We tried but did not succeed.

Note: When a compound verb consists of more than two parts, put a comma after each part, except the last:

jogs, swims, and plays . . .

1. Fire endangers life.
   Fire destroys property.

   _____
   _____

2. I went in.
   I took one look.
   I left.

   _____
   _____

3. A teacher explains the subject.
   A teacher tests students.

   _____
   _____

4. They have money.
   They do not know how to spend it.

   _____
   _____

5. Should we leave?
   Should we wait a little bit longer?

   _____
   _____

6. We closed the windows.
   We turned off the lights.
   We locked the door.

   _____
   _____

7. A good book holds your interest.
   A good book teaches you something.

   _____
   _____

8. He ordered a grilled cheese sandwich.
   He left it untouched.

   _____
   _____

9. The lungs provide the blood with oxygen.
   The lungs remove carbon dioxide.

   _____
   _____

10. She borrowed my notes.
    She did not return them.   _____

                                       _____

Read the following passage. (Sentences have been numbered.)

[1]James and Benjamin Franklin were brothers. [2]They lived and worked in Boston in colonial America. [3]James, the older, operated a printing shop. [4]He employed Benjamin and taught him the printing trade. [5]Often, however, they quarreled and came to blows. [6]Finally, in 1723, Benjamin ran away.

[7]Benjamin arrived in Philadelphia, tired and hungry. [8]He saw a boy eating bread and struck up a conversation. [9]The boy gave Benjamin directions to a baker's shop. [10]Benjamin went there, ordered three pennies' worth of bread, and received three enormous loaves. [11]Their size astounded him. [12]Evidently, bread was much cheaper in Philadelphia than in Boston.

[13]Eating one loaf, Benjamin walked the streets of Philadelphia with another loaf under each arm. [14]He must have looked ridiculous. [15]Deborah Read saw him and laughed. [16]Seven years later, Deborah and Benjamin would become man and wife.

EXERCISE 2. Below, write the subject and the verb of each sentence in the passage you have just read. *Caution:* Some of the subjects are compound, and some of the verbs are compound. The subject and the verb of the first two sentences have been filled in for you as samples.

	SUBJECT	VERB
1.	*James and Benjamin Franklin*	*were*
2.	*They*	*lived and worked*
3.		
4.		
5.		
6.		
7.		
8.		
9.		
10.		

SUBJECT	VERB
11. _____	_____
12. _____	_____
13. _____	_____
14. _____	_____
15. _____	_____
16. _____	_____

Lesson 7 Nouns as Direct Objects

How is the noun *Amy* used in these two sentences?

1. ***Amy*** is our top scorer.
2. The crowd cheered ***Amy***.

In the first sentence, the noun *Amy* is the *subject* of the verb *is*. In the second sentence, the noun *Amy* is the *direct object* of the verb *cheered*.

What Is a Direct Object?

 A *direct object* is a word in the predicate that receives the action of the verb.

In sentence 2, above, the noun *Amy* is the word in the predicate that receives the action of the verb *cheered*. Therefore, the noun *Amy* is the direct object of the verb *cheered*.

Note: There can be no direct object without an action verb.

Compare the noun *Amy* in the following sentences:

1. Our top scorer is ***Amy***.
2. The crowd cheered ***Amy***.

Sentence 1 cannot have a direct object because it has no action verb; *is* does not express action. *Amy,* in sentence 1, is not a direct object.

On the other hand, sentence 2 can have a direct object because it has an action verb; *cheered* expresses action. *Amy,* in sentence 2, receives the action of the verb *cheered* and is a direct object of that verb.

       The crowd cheered ***Amy***.
        S.   V.   D.O.

Question: Are there other verbs, besides *is,* that do not express action?

Answer: Yes. Here are some of them:

am	will be	may be	have been
are	shall be	might be	has been
was	would be	can be	had been
were	should be	could be	will have been

All of the listed verbs, including *is,* are forms of a single verb—the verb *be.*

Remember the following about *am, is, are, will be,* and all other forms of the verb *be:*

1. They do not express action.

2. They cannot have a direct object.

EXERCISE 1.   In which sentence, *a* or *b,* is the italicized noun a direct object? Write the letters **D.O.** on the proper line.

Sample:

a. Paul and Donna are my *cousins.*   *a.* _____

b. I called my *cousins.*   *b.* __D.O._____

1. *a.* Stephen Crane was a *reporter.*   *a.* _____

    b. The publisher dismissed the *reporter.*   *b.* _____

2. *a.* Ginette plays two stringed *instruments.*   *a.* _____

    b. The violin, guitar, and cello are stringed *instruments.*   *b.* _____

3. *a.* Mercedes has been *president* since April.   *a.* _____

    b. The members are blaming the *president.*   *b.* _____

4. *a.* For years Dr. Kroll had been our *dentist.*   *a.* _____

    b. We have found a new *dentist.*   *b.* _____

5. *a.* Mr. Reed is Jean's *teacher.*   *a.* _____

    b. The district has hired a new art *teacher.*   *b.* _____

Easy Procedure for Finding the Direct Object

To find the direct object, ask the question WHAT? or WHOM? right after the action verb.

Question 1:   What is the direct object in the following sentence?
Caroline drives a Ford.

Procedure: Caroline drives a WHAT?

Answer: *Ford* is the direct object.

Question 2:   What is the direct object in the following?
I watched the artist at work.

Procedure: I watched WHOM at work?

Answer: *Artist* is the direct object.

Note that a direct object may be *compound:* **It may consist of more than one word.** The following sentence has a compound direct object:

Heavy rain flooded the ***streets and highways.***
    S.   V.   compound direct object

EXERCISE 2.   In each sentence below, find the verb (**V.**), the subject (**S.**), and the direct object (**D.O.**).

Samples:

Water loosens the soil.	V.	*loosens*
	S.	*Water*
	D.O.	*soil*
The team has already left.	V.	*has left*
	S.	*team*
	D.O.	*none*

1. The speaker's question surprised and amused the audience.

   V. _____
   S. _____
   D.O. _____

2. Have some yogurt and fruit.

   V. _____
   S. _____
   D.O. _____

3. Are the snow and ice melting?

   V. _____
   S. _____
   D.O. _____

4. The World Wide Web and television provide information and entertainment.

   V. _____
   S. _____
   D.O. _____

5. Jonathan returned the books to the library.

   V. _____
   S. _____
   D.O. _____

Lesson 8 Nouns as Indirect Objects

How is the noun *Amy* used in the following sentence?

> The crowd gave **Amy** a cheer.
>   S.   V.   ?   D.O.

Amy is the *indirect object* of the verb *gave.*

What Is an Indirect Object?

 An *indirect object* is a word in the predicate that tells FOR WHOM or TO WHOM something was done, or is being done, or will be done.

Note that there are two nouns after the action verb *gave: Amy* and *cheer.* The noun *cheer* is the *direct object* of *gave* because it answers the question WHAT? (The crowd gave WHAT?) The noun *Amy* tells FOR WHOM the crowd gave a cheer. Therefore, *Amy* is the *indirect object* of the verb *gave.*

> The crowd gave **Amy** a *cheer.*
>   S.   V.   I.O.   D.O.

The above sentence shows that an action verb can have both a *direct object* and an *indirect object* in the same sentence.

Question: Which comes first in a sentence, the direct object or the indirect object?

Answer: The indirect object always comes before the direct object. Note these further examples:

> A friend sent **Marilyn** a *card.*
>   I.O.   D.O.

(*Marilyn* is the indirect object because it tells TO WHOM a friend sent a card.)

Carlos is buying **_Mrs. Lopez_** a _gift_.
                I.O.   D.O.

(_Mrs. Lopez_ is the indirect object because it tells FOR WHOM Carlos is buying a gift.)

The firm pays its **_officers_** a _salary_.
              I.O.   D.O.

(_Officers_ is the indirect object because it tells TO WHOM the firm pays a salary.)

EXERCISE 1.   For each sentence, indicate the verb (**V.**), the subject (**S.**), the indirect object (**I.O.**), if any, and the direct object (**D.O.**), if any.

Samples:

Sunburn itches.		
	V.	_itches_
	S.	_Sunburn_
	I.O.	_none_
	D.O.	_none_

Ms. Jones will tell the court the truth.		
	V.	_will tell_
	S.	_Ms. Jones_
	I.O.	_court_
	D.O.	_truth_

1. The store owner offered the customer a discount.

    V. _____
    S. _____
    I.O. _____
    D.O. _____

2. Did the judge grant the suspect bail?

    V. _____
    S. _____
    I.O. _____
    D.O. _____

3. The city will build the Giants a new stadium.

    V. _____
    S. _____
    I.O. _____
    D.O. _____

4. Brendan has made his parents
a promise.

V. _____

S. _____

I.O. _____

D.O. _____

5. A passerby slipped and fell.

V. _____

S. _____

I.O. _____

D.O. _____

EXERCISE 2. Rewrite the sentence, changing the italicized expression to an indirect object.

Sample:

Did you give the assignment *to Nick?*

  Did you give Nick the assignment? _____

1. Rob gave flowers *to Mia.*

_____

2. Have you ever done a favor *for John?*

_____

3. Liang is lending his science notes *to Kristin.*

_____

4. Rosita is making a blouse *for her sister.*

_____

5. Give the tickets *to the usher.*

_____

6. Who baked a cake *for Jennifer?*

_____

7. Please cut a slice of melon *for Catherine.*

_____

8. Washington is giving emergency aid *to the flooded regions.*

_____

9. I wrote a letter *to Yasmin.*

_____

10. The cashier handed the change *to the customer.*

_____

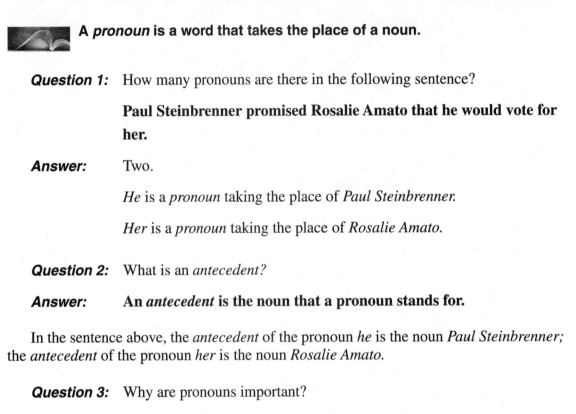

Lesson 9 Pronouns and Antecedents

A *pronoun* is a word that takes the place of a noun.

Question 1: How many pronouns are there in the following sentence?

Paul Steinbrenner promised Rosalie Amato that he would vote for her.

Answer: Two.

He is a *pronoun* taking the place of *Paul Steinbrenner.*

Her is a *pronoun* taking the place of *Rosalie Amato.*

Question 2: What is an *antecedent?*

Answer: **An *antecedent* is the noun that a pronoun stands for.**

In the sentence above, the *antecedent* of the pronoun *he* is the noun *Paul Steinbrenner;* the *antecedent* of the pronoun *her* is the noun *Rosalie Amato.*

Question 3: Why are pronouns important?

Answer: Pronouns make language more smooth and efficient because they let us express ourselves without repetition and in fewer words.

If there were no pronouns, we would have to say:

Paul Steinbrenner promised Rosalie Amato that Paul Steinbrenner would vote for Rosalie Amato.

EXERCISE 1. In the blank space, use a pronoun in place of the italicized antecedent.

Samples:

Joyce has a new *bicycle* but has not used _____*it*_____ .

The gloves are *Karen's*. The muffler is not _____*hers*_____ .

1. Let *the soup* cool before tasting _____.

2. There is *Jeff.* Speak to _____.

3. The magazine is *Tom's,* but the newspaper is not _____.

4. *Chelsea* has nothing to write with. Lend _____ a pen.

5. *Gina* knows that _____ is the next speaker.

6. *Alex and Tony* arrived, but there were no seats for _____.

7. *Joely* did not come because _____ has a cold.

8. If *the tenth grade girls* win today, _____ have a chance for the championship.

9. Has anyone seen *Mike's* notebook? Is that one _____?

10. The stationery was *Ellen's,* and the handwriting was _____, too.

EXERCISE 2. Find the pronoun (**PRON.**) and its antecedent (**ANTECED.**), and write them in the spaces at the right.

Samples:

Sandra said she does not agree.	PRON.	*she*
	ANTECED.	*Sandra*
The Declaration of Independence is an important historical document. It was issued on July 4, 1776.	PRON.	*It*
	ANTECED.	*Declaration of Independence*

1. The challenger knows that he cannot win.

    PRON. _____

    ANTECED. _____

2. Friday was stormy. It was a miserable day.

    PRON. _____

    ANTECED. _____

3. Ask Eric and Anna if they can come.

    PRON. _____

    ANTECED. _____

4. Not one motel had a vacancy; each was booked to capacity.

    PRON. _____

    ANTECED. _____

5. "We want a hit!" yelled the fans.

PRON. _____

ANTECED. _____

6. Jess complained: "Sam has not invited me."

PRON. _____

ANTECED. _____

7. Mr. Walsh told the clerk: "I always pay cash."

PRON. _____

ANTECED. _____

8. The committee asks: "Help us make this town a better place to live in."

PRON. _____

ANTECED. _____

Composition Hint

To avoid repeating a noun you have just mentioned, use a pronoun.

INSTEAD OF: I know Texas well because Texas is my home state.

WRITE: I know Texas well because *it* is my home state.

The pronoun *it* enables you to avoid repeating the noun *Texas.*

EXERCISE 3.   What pronoun can you use to avoid repeating the italicized word or words? Write your answer in the space provided.

Sample:

We did not invite Grace, though *Grace* would have liked to come.   *she*

1. The ball landed right in your hands, but you could not hold on to *the ball.*   _____

2. The jacket is Fahim's and the sweater is *Fahim's,* too.   _____

3. Julie and Audrey are our friends. We have nothing against *Julie and Audrey.*   _____

4. They looked for chocolate chip cookie dough ice cream, but *chocolate chip cookie dough ice cream* was not on the menu.   _____

5. Ask the bus driver. *The bus driver* will be only too glad to help you.   _____

Personal Pronouns

The personal pronouns are

 I, you, he, she, it, we, they.

They are called ***personal pronouns*** because, except for *it*, they all refer to *persons*.

These pronouns are among the most troublesome words in our language.

Question: Why are the personal pronouns troublesome?

Answer: Most of these pronouns change in form, depending on the way they are used in a sentence. On the other hand, the nouns that these pronouns stand for do not change.

For example, take the noun *George.* We can use *George* as either a subject, a direct object, or an indirect object.

    George can be a SUBJECT: ***George*** complained.
                                                                    S.   V.

    George can be a DIRECT OBJECT: The noise bothered ***George.***
                                                                 S.   V.   D.O.

    George can be an INDIRECT OBJECT: The noise gave ***George*** a headache.
                                                              S.   V.   I.O.   D.O.

Obviously, the noun *George* does not change in form, whether used as a subject, a direct object, or an indirect object.

But most pronouns change in form, depending on their use. For example, *he* can be used as a subject, but *not* as a direct object or an indirect object.

    He can be a SUBJECT: ***He*** complained.
                                                                     S.   V.

    For a DIRECT OBJECT, we must use *him:*   The noise bothered ***him.***
                                                                   S.   V.   D.O.

    Also, for an INDIRECT OBJECT we must use *him:*   The noise gave ***him*** a headache.
                                                                    S.   V.   I.O.   D.O.

The Different Forms of the Personal Pronouns

If we need a pronoun as a SUBJECT, we can use one of the following:

    I   you   he   she   it   we   they

If we need a pronoun as a DIRECT OBJECT or an INDIRECT OBJECT, we can use one of the following:

me   **you**   **him**   **her**   **it**   **us**   **them**

If we need a pronoun TO SHOW POSSESSION, we can use one of the following:

my,	**your,**	**his**	**her,**	**its**	**our,**	**their,**
mine	**yours**		**hers**		**ours**	**theirs**

Note: Only *you* and *it* have the same form for subject, direct object, and indirect object.

EXERCISE 1.   Supply the missing pronoun.

Samples:

Brianna likes music. _____*She*_____ plays the guitar.

It was Jim. I recognized _____*him*_____ .

This book must be Pedro's. It is definitely _____*his*_____ .

1. Isabella and I are neighbors. _____ live on the same street.

2. Melanie and Abe are our friends. We like _____.

3. Ellen and I will come when you call _____.

4. Mr. and Mrs. Stern have just made the last mortgage payment. Now the house is all _____.

5. I admit I am to blame. The fault is _____.

Pronouns in Combinations

Pronouns and nouns may be combined to form compound subjects, compound indirect objects, and compound direct objects.

<u>**Corey and I**</u> attended.   (COMPOUND SUBJECT)
  compound S.

Peter showed <u>**Corey and me**</u> the pictures.   (COMPOUND INDIRECT OBJECT)
          compound I.O.

The instructor chose <u>**Corey and me.**</u>   (COMPOUND DIRECT OBJECT)
          compound D.O.

Composition Hint

Make your writing more interesting and effective by removing unnecessary words. Note how compound subjects, compound indirect objects, and compound direct objects can help.

INSTEAD OF: My friends liked the movie. I liked the movie.

WRITE: ***My friends and I*** liked the movie.
          compound S.

INSTEAD OF: You gave Kelly the wrong directions. You gave us the wrong directions.

WRITE: You gave ***Kelly and us*** the wrong directions.
          compound I.O.

INSTEAD OF: She invited her cousin. She invited me.

WRITE: She invited ***her cousin and me.***
          compound D.O.

EXERCISE 2.   Rewrite each pair of sentences as one sentence, taking out the unnecessary words. Your new sentence should contain a compound subject, compound indirect object, or compound direct object.

Sample:

Andrea asked several questions. I asked several questions.

Andrea and I asked several questions.

1. My friend joined the swimming team. I joined the swimming team.

2. Diane met my cousin at the game. Diane met me at the game.

3. Shawn will go to the meeting. She will go to the meeting.

4. The state university offered Bill a scholarship. The state university offered Tori a scholarship.

5. Our opponents have had a good season. We have had a good season.

   _____

6. They have known the Russos a long time. They have known us a long time.

   _____

7. My sister saw the latest *Lord of the Rings* movie. He saw the latest *Lord of the Rings* movie.

   _____

8. Evan gave Jack the wrong phone number. Evan gave me the wrong phone number.

   _____

9. Caitlin heard the crash down the hall. I heard the crash down the hall.

   _____

10. Lindsay gave Ted her best smile. Lindsay gave us her best smile.

   _____

Pronouns in Contractions

As we noted in Lesson 3, page 19,

 A *contraction* is a combination of two words with one or more letters omitted. An *apostrophe* ['] takes the place of the omitted letters.

PRONOUN	+	VERB	=	CONTRACTION	LETTER(S) OMITTED
you	+	are	=	*you're*	*a*
she	+	will	=	*she'll*	*w i*
I	+	would	=	*I'd*	*w o u l*

Note that the first word in a contraction does not lose any letters—only the second one does. In the following contraction, the pronoun *us* loses a letter because it is the second word.

   let + us = *let's*

Contractions are commonly used in conversation and in friendly letters and notes. Study the following contractions:

it	+	is	=	*it's*		I	+	am	=	*I'm*
they	+	will	=	*they'll*		we	+	are	=	*we're*
you	+	have	=	*you've*		he	+	would	=	*he'd*

EXERCISE 1. A contraction stands for two words. Write the two words for each italicized contraction below.

Sample:

He'll go.   =   <u>He will</u>

1. *You'd* laugh!   =   _____

2. *They've* left.   =   _____

3. *Let's* stop.   =   _____

4. *They're* clever.   =   _____

5. *It's* a pity.   =   _____

EXERCISE 2. Write each of the following as a contraction.

Sample:

they will   =   *they'll*

1. let us   =   _____   6. you would   =   _____

2. you have   =   _____   7. we have   =   _____

3. they are   =   _____   8. I am   =   _____

4. we will   =   _____   9. they would   =   _____

5. it is   =   _____   10. you are   =   _____

Caution: Do not confuse a contraction with a possessive pronoun.

A contraction *always* has an apostrophe:

you'll (you will); **it's** (it is), etc.

A possessive pronoun *never* has an apostrophe:

yours, his, hers, its, ours, theirs

CONTRACTIONS	POSSESSIVE PRONOUNS
(*Use an apostrophe to replace omitted letters.*)	(*Do not use an apostrophe.*)
It's (It is) raining.	***Its*** fur is soft.
You're (You are) wrong.	***Your*** friend is here.
They're (They are) here.	***Their*** parents came.

EXERCISE 3.   Write the choice that makes the sentence correct.

Samples:

The employees want (*they're, their*) pay.   _their_

Note that ***they're*** would not fit because it means *they are*.

You know (*they're, their*) not happy.   _they're_

Note that ***they're*** (*they are*) fits in with the rest of the sentence.

1. Do they have (*they're, their*) uniforms?   _____

2. By now (*they're, their*) really tired.   _____

3. Are these (*you're, your*) notes?   _____

4. (*It's, Its*) too late.   _____

5. Is the laptop computer (*her's, hers*)?   _____

6. This is my book. Where is (*yours, your's*)?   _____

7. The cat hurt (*its, it's*) tail.   _____

8. Shall we go to your house after school or (*our's, ours*)?   _____

9. (*Your, You're*) always complaining.   _____

10. (*Lets, Let's*) go!   _____

Lesson 10 Review of Verbs, Nouns, and Pronouns

To learn what part of speech a word is, ask yourself: How is the word used in its sentence?

For example, in sentence 1 below, *paper* is a noun; it names a thing. In sentence 2, paper is a verb; it expresses action.

1. I need more ***paper***.
      N.

2. The room will look better if we ***paper*** the walls.
                                              V.

EXERCISE 1. Like many words in English, each of the following can be a noun or a verb, depending on how it is used in a sentence. For each word, write two sentences—one using the word as a noun and the other using the word as a verb.

Sample:

bridge/bridge

We are about ready to cross the longest *bridge* in the state.

Gillian *bridges* the gap in age by taking an interest in her little sister's dolls.

1. hound/hound

   _____

   _____

2. monitor/monitor

   _____

   _____

3. train/train

   _____

   _____

4. effect/effect

_____

_____

5. hedge/hedge

_____

_____

As you do these exercises, remember that verbs can be more than one word.

Question: Is the verb in the following sentence *mailed* or *have been mailed?*
The letters have been mailed.

Answer: *have been mailed.*

Note: Whenever you are asked for the verb of a sentence containing a verb phrase, *give the whole verb phrase.*

EXERCISE 2.   Name the verb in each of the following sentences.

Sample:

They must have lost their way.   *must have lost* _____

1. Anything can happen.   _____

2. You might have tried harder.   _____

3. Is the trash being removed?   _____

4. They should have been invited.   _____

5. Jack should have been given another chance.   _____

6. Elizabeth reads a book in a day.   _____

7. Are we here yet?   _____

8. Colleen is studying physics.   _____

Nouns can be tricky, too. They change form depending on how they are used—as singular, plural, or possessive nouns. On the next page is a summary of the rules for forming plurals of nouns.

When to add *s*:

A. To most nouns: book—books. (See Rule 1, page 28.)

A–X. *Exceptions to A:*

man—men	foot—feet	mouse—mice
woman—women	tooth—teeth	goose—geese
child—children	louse—lice	ox—oxen

(See Rule 2 Exceptions, page 28.)

B. To most nouns ending in *f:* belief—beliefs. (See Rule 3, page 30.)

B–X. *Exceptions to B:*

leaf—leaves	shelf—shelves
loaf—loaves	thief—thieves
half—halves	wolf—wolves
self—selves	

C. To nouns ending in a *vowel + y:* way—ways. (See Rule 5, page 31.)

D. To nouns ending in a *vowel + o:* radio—radios. (See Rule 7, page 33.)

E. To most nouns ending in a *consonant + o:* auto—autos. (See Rule 8, page 33.)

When to add *es*:

E–X. *Exceptions to E:*

potato + es = potatoes	echo + es = echoes
tomato + es = tomatoes	veto + es = vetoes

F. To nouns ending in   *s:* class + es = classes
                  sh: wish + es = wishes
                  ch: bench + es = benches
              or *x:* box + es = boxes

(See Rule 2, page 28.)

When to change *y* to *i* and add *es*:

G. When a noun ends in a *consonant + y*: lady—ladies. (See Rule 6, page 31.)

When to change *f* to *v* and add *s*:

H. In the following three nouns ending in *fe* and their compounds:

knife—knives
life—lives
wife—wives
penknife—penknives
housewife—housewives
(See Rule 4, page 30.)

EXERCISE 3. For each singular noun below, write (*a*) the plural and (*b*) the *letter* of the rule for forming that plural. Take your rule letters from the preceding four boxes.

Samples:

SINGULAR	PLURAL	RULE LETTER
notebook	*notebooks*	*A*
penknife	*penknives*	*H*
tax	*taxes*	*F*
baby	*babies*	*G*
ox	*oxen*	*A–X*

1. pencil
2. leaf
3. child
4. tomato
5. louse
6. piano
7. sheriff
8. torch
9. echo
10. party
11. landlady
12. woman
13. jackknife
14. alloy
15. dash
16. stepchild
17. rodeo

18. life _____ _____

19. pie _____ _____

20. monkey _____ _____

EXERCISE 4.   As we have learned, a noun may have as many as four forms.

(1)	(2)	(3)	(4)
		POSSESSIVE	POSSESSIVE
SINGULAR	PLURAL	SINGULAR	PLURAL
student	students	student's	students'

On each line below, only one form of a noun is given. Write the other three forms of that noun.

SINGULAR	PLURAL	POSSESSIVE SINGULAR	POSSESSIVE PLURAL
1. girl	_____	_____	_____
2. _____	children	_____	_____
3. _____	teachers	_____	_____
4. _____	_____	nurse's	_____
5. _____	_____	_____	women's

Read the following. (Sentences have been numbered.)

[1]J. R. R. Tolkien creates a complex fictional world, Middle Earth, in his trilogy of books, *The Lord of the Rings.* [2]He called the first book *The Fellowship of the Ring.* [3]In this book, Sauron is the Dark Lord of Mordor who derived his power from the One Ring. [4]He wished to enslave Middle Earth by using the One Ring but lost it before he could accomplish his goal. [5]Through odd twists of circumstances, the ring comes to a hobbit called Frodo Baggins. [6]He and some friends form the Fellowship and begin a journey to take the ring to the Cracks of Doom in the mountain Oroduin, inside Sauron's realm. [7]It is the only place where it can be destroyed.

[8]Frodo and friends have many adventures. [9]They are chased by Ringwraiths, they pass through the Misty Mountains, and they proceed to Lorien, where Lady Galadriel lives. [10]Here she tests them and gives them gifts. [11]Eventually, Frodo decides his quest must lead him to Mordor, and he leaves secretly to continue it alone.

continued

12Though tales of fantasy, the *Lord of the Rings* books do echo truths about the real world we live in. 13They will bring you hours of great reading.

EXERCISE 5.   Write the antecedents of the pronouns listed below.

Sample:

He (sentence 2)   <u>J. R. R. Tolkien   </u>

1. *He* (sentence 4)   _____

2. *it* (sentence 4)   _____

3. *It* (sentence 7)   _____

4. *it* (sentence 7)   _____

5. *They* (sentence 9)   _____

6. *she* (sentence 10)   _____

7. *them* (sentence 10)   _____

8. *him* (sentence 11)   _____

9. *it* (sentence 11)   _____

10. *They* (sentence 13)   _____

Note: In sentence 7, the two occurrences of *it*, with different antecedents, might make for confusing reading. It is better to change one *it* back to what it refers to. For example, change the second *it* to *the ring*.

EXERCISE 6.   Write:

1. the subject of the verb *comes* in sentence 5: _____

2. the direct object of the verb *gives* in sentence 10: _____

3. the indirect object of the verb *gives* in sentence 10: _____

4. the subject of the verb *do echo* in sentence 12: _____

5. the direct object of the verb *will bring* in sentence 13: _____

6. the indirect object of the verb *will bring* in sentence 13: _____

EXERCISE 7.   List 10 proper nouns and 10 common nouns from the passage.

PROPER   COMMON

1. _____   _____

2. _____   _____

3. _____   _____

4. _____   _____

5. _____   _____

6. _____   _____

7. _____   _____

8. _____   _____

9. _____   _____

10. _____   _____

Recall that in less formal writing and conversation, contractions may be used.

EXERCISE 8.   Which contraction *beginning with a pronoun* can replace the italicized words? Write your answer in the space provided.

Samples:

You are wasting time.   _You're_ _____

Ask her where *the teams are* playing.   _they're_ _____

1. *We would* be glad to go along.   _____

2. Do you know if *he is* home?   _____

3. *My friends and I will* help you.   _____

4. *You have* no time to lose.   _____

5. *Terry will* be there.   _____

Lesson 11 Adjectives

What is the difference between *sweater* and *that white turtleneck sweater?*

Sweater means any sweater at all. *That, white,* and *turtleneck* **modify** (change) the meaning of *sweater* from any sweater to one particular sweater. These words are *adjectives.*

What Is an *Adjective?*

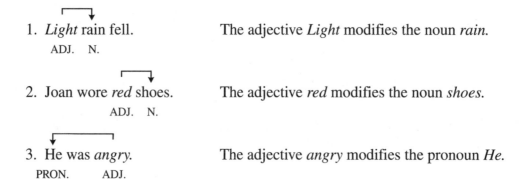

An *adjective* is a word that modifies a noun or a pronoun.

Here are some more examples:

1. *Light* rain fell.
   ADJ. N.

   The adjective *Light* modifies the noun *rain.*

2. Joan wore *red* shoes.
       ADJ. N.

   The adjective *red* modifies the noun *shoes.*

3. He was *angry.*
   PRON.   ADJ.

   The adjective *angry* modifies the pronoun *He.*

Adjectives give information by answering such questions as *What kind? Which one? How many? Whose?*

WHAT KIND?	*blue* sky, *rainy* day, *early* riser
WHICH ONE?	*this* book, *first* job, *second* floor
HOW MANY?	*four* girls, *many* reasons, *few* failures
WHOSE?	*my* brother, *your* face, *his* wallet

Question: How many adjectives are there in the following?
Two husky, rough-coated dogs trotted out as we approached the farmhouse, and we called to them in a friendly way, but they were watchful and suspicious.

Answer: Eight.

---

1. *Two,*
2. *husky,* and
3. *rough-coated*   modify the noun *dogs;*
4. *the*   modifies the noun *farmhouse;*
5. *a* and
6. *friendly*   modify the noun *way;*
7. *watchful* and
8. *suspicious*   modify the pronoun *they.*

Note: *The*, *a,* and *an,* the most frequently encountered of all adjectives, are called **articles.** Since they appear so often, we can agree to exclude them when identifying adjectives.

EXERCISE 1.   In each sentence below, find an adjective and explain what it modifies.

Samples:

We sat in the first row.

ADJ.   *first*   modifies   *N. row* .

She was unhappy.

ADJ.   *unhappy*   modifies   *PRON. She* .

1. They were early.

    ADJ. _____   modifies _____

2. Ted had no money.

    ADJ. _____   modifies _____

3. Two birds flew into the trees.

    ADJ. _____   modifies _____

4. Are the rolls fresh?

    ADJ. _____   modifies _____

5. You look pale.

    ADJ. _____   modifies _____

6. The noise was ear-splitting.

    ADJ. _____   modifies _____

7. Warmer weather is on the way.

    ADJ. _____   modifies _____

8. The results were poor.

   ADJ. _____ modifies _____

9. Sue has three brothers.

   ADJ. _____ modifies _____

10. Thirty people applied for the job.

    ADJ. _____ modifies _____

Proper Adjectives

Recall from Lesson 4, page 24, that proper nouns (*Canada, Shakespeare,* etc.) are cap-italized. The adjectives formed from proper nouns (*Canadian, Shakespearean,* etc.) gener-ally are capitalized, too. They are called ***proper adjectives.*** Here are some proper nouns and the proper adjectives that can be formed from them.

PROPER NOUN	PROPER ADJECTIVE
China	*Chinese* food
Jefferson	*Jeffersonian* democracy
Egypt	*Egyptian* pyramids
France	*French* perfume
Rome	*Roman* arch

Composition Hint

Make your writing more concise by replacing a wordy expression with an adjective.

WORDY: The diplomat visited several nations *on the continent of Africa.*

CONCISE: The diplomat visited several ***African*** nations.
                          ADJ.

WORDY: Avoid decisions *that are made in haste.*

CONCISE: Avoid ***hasty*** decisions.
                  ADJ.

EXERCISE 2.   Rewrite the sentence, using an adjective instead of the italicized expression.

Sample:

Many dealers sell products *manufactured in Japan.*

   Many dealers sell Japanese products. _____

---

1. *Olives imported from Spain* are sold in supermarkets.

   _____

2. They spoke in words *that were full of bitterness.*

   _____

3. I read an article on the Internet about Inuits *who live in Canada.*

   _____

4. Coffee *grown in Brazil* is flavorful.

   _____

5. He never makes a move *that involves risk.*

   _____

6. Many gifts *made by hand* are deeply appreciated.

   _____

7. In every class there are students *who give in to laziness.*

   _____

8. What is the name of the ambassador *from the Commonwealth of Australia?*

   _____

Another Composition Hint

Before using an adjective, make sure that it is needed.

QUESTION: What is wrong with the following sentence?
We want the true facts.

ANSWER: The adjective *true* is not needed because all facts are true. The sentence should read:
We want the facts.

EXERCISE 3.   Which adjectives should be removed because they are unnecessary?

Sample:

Put some cold ice cubes into the lemonade.   *cold*_____

1. I was a stupid fool.   _____

2. A young, rich millionaire has bought the painting. _____

ADJECTIVES   71

3. We were never told the real truth.

_____

4. Antony wept at the sight of Caesar's dead corpse.

_____

5. Draw a round circle.

_____

6. The end result was that we lost the game.

_____

7. Do you own any old antiques?

_____

8. One student slept throughout the entire assembly.

_____

9. It happened on a summer evening in July.

_____

10. A cold icy wind is blowing from the northeast.

_____

Predicate Adjectives and Predicate Nouns

In some sentences, all we need to make a complete statement is a subject and a verb.

> Birds fly.
> S.   V.

> John smiled.
> S.   V.

But in other sentences, a subject and a verb may not be enough, especially if the verb is a linking verb.

> The milk *tastes* . . .
> S. L.V.

> Andy *is* . . .
> S. L.V.

In each of the above two sentences, we must add a **complement—a "completing" word or expression**—to the linking verb. For example:

> The milk tastes *sour.*
>   L.V.

> (The adjective *sour* is a *complement*
> of the linking verb *tastes*.)

Andy is the ***owner.***
                L.V.

(The noun *owner* is a *complement*
of the linking verb *is*.)

EXERCISE 1.   Add a suitable complement to each linking verb below to complete
the sentence. You may choose your complements from the following list:

louder	tall	delicious	criminals
water	painters	islands	

Sample:

Oranges *are*   _juicy_____.
          L.V.

1. Oaks *grow* _____.
         L.V.

2. Thieves *are* _____.
           L.V.

3. The cake *looked* _____.
            L.V.

4. Ice *becomes* _____.
        L.V.

5. Rembrandt and Picasso *were* _____.
                    L.V.

6. Iceland and Greenland *are* _____.
                    L.V.

    In the exercise you have just done, you used six complements to complete six linking
verbs. No doubt you have been using complements all your life without knowing that they
were complements.
    There are several kinds of complements. Here we study two of them:

    1. the *predicate adjective,* and

    2. the *predicate noun.*

PREDICATE ADJECTIVES

What Is a Predicate Adjective?

A *predicate adjective* is an adjective that completes a linking verb and modifies the subject of that linking verb.

Here are two examples of predicate adjectives:

The soup *tastes* **salty.**
 S. L.V. PRED. ADJ.

(*Salty* is a predicate adjective because it completes the linking verb *tastes* and modifies the subject *soup*.)

You *were* **fabulous.**
 S. L.V. PRED. ADJ.

(*Fabulous* is a predicate adjective because it completes the linking verb *were* and modifies the subject *You*.)

EXERCISE 2.   In each sentence below, find the *linking verb,* the *predicate adjective,* and the word that the predicate adjective *modifies*.

Samples:

The children grew restless.	L.V.	*grew*
	PRED. ADJ.	*restless*
	MODIFIES	*children*
She has been helpful.	L.V.	*has been*
	PRED. ADJ.	*helpful*
	MODIFIES	*She*
1. The cellar smells damp.	L.V.	
	PRED. ADJ.	
	MODIFIES	
2. Their story sounded strange.	L.V.	
	PRED. ADJ.	
	MODIFIES	

3. Laura looked annoyed.   L.V.   _____

                                    PRED. ADJ.   _____

                                    MODIFIES   _____

4. Your appetite seems good.   L.V.   _____

                                    PRED. ADJ.   _____

                                    MODIFIES   _____

5. He must have been angry.   L.V.   _____

                                    PRED. ADJ.   _____

                                    MODIFIES   _____

PREDICATE NOUNS

What Is a Predicate Noun?

A *predicate noun* is a noun that completes a linking verb and explains the subject of that linking verb.

Here is an example:

Tara *is* my ***cousin***.
S.   L.V.   PRED. N.

(*Cousin* is a predicate noun because it completes the linking verb *is* and explains the subject *Tara*.)

Here are some further examples of predicate nouns.

A kitten *becomes* a ***cat***.
S.   L.V.   PRED. N.

The experiment *was* a ***failure***.
S.   L.V.   PRED. N.

EXERCISE 3.   In each of the following sentences, find the *subject*, the *linking verb*, and the *predicate noun* that explains the subject.

Sample:

Australia is a continent.   SUBJ.   *Australia* _____

                                    L.V.   *is* _____

                                    PRED. N.   *continent* _____

ADJECTIVES   **75**

1. Copper is a metal.

SUBJ. _____

L.V. _____

PRED. N. _____

2. Was Marie the umpire?

SUBJ. _____

L.V. _____

PRED. N. _____

3. Julio has been captain for a year.

SUBJ. _____

L.V. _____

PRED. N. _____

4. That exam should have been a breeze.

SUBJ. _____

L.V. _____

PRED. N. _____

5. The pizza will be our lunch.

SUBJ. _____

L.V. _____

PRED. N. _____

Composition Hint

We often have a choice when we explain or describe a subject: We can use either (1) a predicate noun or (2) a predicate adjective.

1. I was a *fool.*
   PRED. N.

   (The predicate noun *fool* describes the subject *I.*)

2. I was *foolish.*
   PRED. ADJ.

   (The predicate adjective *foolish* describes the subject *I.*)

Become familiar with both choices. Then, when you write, you will be able to select the one that better expresses your idea in a particular situation.

EXERCISE 4. Rewrite each sentence, changing the predicate noun to a predicate adjective.

Sample:

Joan is a wonder.

Joan is wonderful.

1. The play was a success.

_____

2. Pete has never been a friend.

_____

3. My desk is a mess.

_____

4. The news was a surprise.

_____

5. Was the outcome a shock?

_____

6. David's new band is a sensation.

_____

7. It was a custom to have homecoming at the last game of the season.

_____

8. Because she worked out every day, her legs were solid muscle.

_____

9. The design of the new music room was the shape of a circle.

_____

10. The entire trip was a nightmare.

_____

EXERCISE 5.   Rewrite each sentence, changing the predicate adjective to a predicate noun.

Sample:

Ben was sensational.

Ben was a sensation.

1. You were cowardly.

2. Gambling can be risky.

3. He was brutal.

4. The puppy is beautiful.

5. Don't be bossy.

6. They said the man in the blue baseball cap was creepy.

7. It was pitiful to see him this way.

8. Their meeting was coincidental.

9. The loss of the running back was catastrophic.

10. Driving under the influence of alcohol is felonious.

Lesson 12 Adverbs

If some reporter were to describe the weather for us by saying,

"It snowed,"

we would not be entirely satisfied. We would want to know the answers to certain questions:

1. *How,* or *to what extent,* did it snow?
2. *When* did it snow?
3. *Where* did it snow?

Words that tell *how, when,* or *where* are adverbs.

If our reporter had answered the above questions by using some adverbs—for example, if he or she had said,

"It snowed *heavily yesterday upstate,*"

we would have had a better idea of the weather.

What Is an Adverb?

An *adverb* is a word that modifies either
a verb, or
an adjective, or
another adverb.

We now look at these uses of an adverb one at a time.

I. An adverb is a word that modifies a verb.

The Pirates *played **brilliantly.***   (*Brilliantly* is an adverb because it modifies
            V.   ADV.   the verb *played*.)

The team *performed **well.***   (*Well* is an adverb because it modifies the
          V.   ADV.   verb *performed*.)

The Dodgers *did **not** play.*   (*Not* is an adverb because it modifies the
        V. ADV. V.   verb *did play*.)

ADVERBS

They *are playing* **tomorrow**.
    V.   ADV.

(*Tomorrow* is an adverb because it modifies the verb *are playing*.)

They *will play* **here**.
    V.   ADV.

(*Here* is an adverb because it modifies the verb *will play*.)

Most adverbs answer one of the following questions: HOW? WHEN? WHERE? TO WHAT EXTENT?

The Pirates played **brilliantly**.
                  ADV.

(*Brilliantly* tells HOW the Pirates played.)

They are playing **tomorrow**.
             ADV.

(*Tomorrow* tells WHEN they are playing.)

They will play **here**.
          ADV.

(*Here* tells WHERE they will play.)

They have **fully** recovered from
         ADV.
their slump.

(*Fully* tells TO WHAT EXTENT they have recovered.)

EXERCISE 1. Find the adverb and the verb that it modifies.

Sample:

Your money will be refunded immediately.

The ADV. ___*immediately*___ modifies
the V. ___*will be refunded*___ .

1. The damage was repaired quickly.

The ADV. _____ modifies
the V. _____ .

2. Bill usually brings his lunch.

The ADV. _____ modifies
the V. _____ .

3. The car stopped suddenly.

The ADV. _____ modifies
the V. _____ .

4. We are leaving soon.

The ADV. _____ modifies
the V. _____ .

5. The locker door sometimes sticks.

The ADV. _____ modifies
the V. _____ .

6. Look in the closet. Is your coat there?

The ADV. _____ modifies
the V. _____ .

7. Justine has not completed her test.

The ADV. _____ modifies

the V. _____ .

8. Remove the cover carefully.

The ADV. _____ modifies

the V. _____ .

9. Did the exchange students stay long?

The ADV. _____ modifies

the V. _____ .

10. Rarely does Jay fall off his skateboard.

The ADV. _____ modifies

the V. _____ .

II. An adverb is a word that modifies an adjective.

A *very odd* thing happened.
   ADV. ADJ.

(*Very* is an adverb because it modifies the adjective *odd*.)

The cobra is a ***highly*** *poisonous* snake.
        ADV.   ADJ.

(*Highly* is an adverb because it modifies the adjective *poisonous*.)

A window was ***partly*** *open*.
        ADV. ADJ.

(*Partly* is an adverb because it modifies the predicate adjective *open*.)

EXERCISE 2. Find the adverb and the adjective that it modifies.

Sample:

You were absolutely right.

The ADV. *absolutely* modifies

the ADJ. *right* .

1. They were very lucky.

The ADV. _____ modifies

the ADJ. _____ .

2. An unusually large crowd gathered.

The ADV. _____ modifies

the ADJ. _____ .

3. Is the soup too hot?

The ADV. _____ modifies

the ADJ. _____ .

4. They had a quite inexpensive meal.

The ADV. _____ modifies

the ADJ. _____ .

5. Freshly made pasta tastes fantastic.

The ADV. _____ modifies

the ADJ. _____ .

III. An adverb is a word that modifies another adverb.

The fight began **_quite_** _unexpectedly_. (*Quite* is an adverb because it modi-
                ADV.   ADV.   fies the adverb *unexpectedly*.)

I **_very_** _quietly_ closed the door. (*Very* is an adverb because it modifies
  ADV. ADV.   the adverb *quietly*.)

Both teams played **_extremely_** _well_. (*Extremely* is an adverb because it
              ADV.   ADV.   modifies the adverb *well*.)

EXERCISE 3. Find the two adverbs in the sentence, and explain why each is an adverb.

Sample:

Our plants are doing
extremely well.

(*a*) ___*Extremely*___ is an adverb because
it modifies the ___*adv. well*___ .

(*b*) ___*Well*___ is an adverb because
it modifies the ___*v. are doing*___ .

1. You reported the details quite
accurately.

(*a*) _____ is an adverb because
it modifies the _____ .

(*b*) _____ is an adverb because
it modifies the _____ .

2. Alex very cleverly kept out
of the argument.

(*a*) _____ is an adverb because
it modifies the _____ .

(*b*) _____ is an adverb because
it modifies the _____ .

3. Lightning flashed and rain fell
shortly afterward.

(*a*) _____ is an adverb because
it modifies the _____ .

(*b*) _____ is an adverb because
it modifies the _____ .

4. He swings at the ball too soon.

(*a*) _____ is an adverb because
it modifies the _____ .

(*b*) _____ is an adverb because
it modifies the _____ .

5. I left at noon, but Sherry
   had left somewhat earlier.

   (a) _____ is an adverb because

   it modifies the _____ .

   (b) _____ is an adverb because

   it modifies the _____ .

Summary: **An adverb is a word that modifies**

a verb, or

an adjective, or

another adverb.

EXERCISE 4.   Explain why the italicized word is an adverb.

Samples:

You acted *wisely*.   <u>Wisely</u> modifies the <u>v. acted</u> .

You acted *very* wisely.   <u>Very</u> modifies the <u>adv. wisely</u> .

You were *very* wise.   <u>Very</u> modifies the <u>adj. wise</u> .

1. She poured the soup *carefully*.   _____ modifies the _____ .

2. She poured *quite* carefully.   _____ modifies the _____ .

3. She was *quite* careful.   _____ modifies the _____ .

4. The apple was *partly* rotten.   _____ modifies the _____ .

5. They behaved *strangely*.   _____ modifies the _____ .

6. I was *so* angry.   _____ modifies the _____ .

7. Please walk *more* slowly.   _____ modifies the _____ .

8. The quarrel has *not* ended.   _____ modifies the _____ .

9. Were you *really* afraid?   _____ modifies the _____ .

10. Do not begin *too* suddenly.   _____ modifies the _____ .

Forming Adverbs from Adjectives

I. Most adverbs are formed by adding *ly* to an adjective.

ADJECTIVE   ADVERB

skillful   + ly = skillfully
brave   + ly = bravely

In some cases, however, as in II and III that follow, we must make a change in the adjective before adding *ly*.

II. If an adjective ends in *ic*, add *al* before adding *ly*.

basic   + al + ly = basically

terrific + al + ly = terrifically

III. If an adjective ends in *y*, change the *y* to *i* and then add *ly*.

easy ⟶ [easi] + ly = easily

noisy ⟶ [noisi] + ly = noisily

IV. If an adjective ends in *le*, do not add *ly*; simply change *le* to *ly*.

able   ⟶ ably

gentle ⟶ gently

EXERCISE 1.   Change the following adjectives to adverbs.

Samples:

ADVERB   ADJECTIVE

wise   *wisely*

lazy   *lazily*

1. courageous _____

2. fierce   _____

3. final   _____

4. economic   _____

5. annual   _____

6. steady   _____

7. favorable   _____

8. scientific _____

9. possible _____

10. comfortable _____

EXERCISE 2.　Change the following adverbs to adjectives.

Samples:

ADVERB	ADJECTIVE
definitely	*definite*
ably	*able*

1. gradually _____

2. unluckily _____

3. unfortunately _____

4. basically _____

5. simply _____

Composition Hint _____

Adverbs can often help us express ourselves more concisely. Compare the following:

WORDY:　You worked ***in a careless manner***.

CONCISE:　You worked ***carelessly***.

EXERCISE 3.　Express the following thoughts more concisely. *Hint:* Change the italicized expression to an adverb ending in **ly.**

Samples:

The motor runs *with a noisy sound.*

　The motor runs noisily.
_____

Under normal conditions, we leave at 3 P.M.

　Normally, we leave at 3 P.M.
_____

1. They behaved *in a strange way.*

_____

ADVERBS　　　　　　　　　　　　　　　　　　　　**85**

2. *Under usual circumstances,* the school bus is on time.

_____

3. He acted *like a foolish person.*

_____

4. *All of a sudden,* the lights went out.

_____

5. My heart was beating *at a rapid rate.*

_____

6. *It is probable that* you will soon feel better.

_____

7. Our meetings are run *in a democratic way.*

_____

8. *In an angry voice,* she demanded that we leave at once.

_____

9. Try to explain the problem *in simple language.*

_____

10. *From a financial point of view,* the business is sound.

_____

Recognizing Adverbs and Adjectives

I. A word is not an adverb just because it ends in **ly.** To tell whether or not a particular word is an adverb, we must see how that word is used in its sentence.

Question 1: Is *weekly* an adverb in this sentence?

1. The workers receive a *weekly* salary.

Answer: No.

Reason: *Weekly* modifies the noun *salary*. A word that modifies a noun is an *adjective*. Therefore, *weekly,* in sentence 1, is an *adjective.*

Question 2: Is *weekly* an adverb in the following sentence?

2. The workers are paid *weekly.*

Answer: Yes.

Reason: *Weekly* modifies the verb *are paid*. A word that modifies a verb is an adverb. Therefore, in sentence 2, *weekly* is an *adverb*.

EXERCISE 1.   Is the italicized word an adverb or an adjective? *Hint:* Before giving your answer, check to see how the italicized word is used in its sentence.

Samples:

Today the mail came *early*.   <u>*adverb*</u>

We had an *early* dinner.   <u>*adjective*</u>

1. We pay the cell phone bill *monthly*.   _____

2. How much is your *monthly* cell phone bill?   _____

3. Do you read a newspaper *daily?*   _____

4. Susan's dad left for his *daily* trip to the office.   _____

5. What is the minimum *hourly* wage?   _____

6. The patient's temperature was checked *hourly*. _____

II. Some words that do not end in *ly*—for example, *long* and *fast*—can be adverbs or adjectives. Again, we must see how such words are used in their sentences before saying that they are adverbs or adjectives.

Question 1:   Is *long* an adverb in this sentence?

1. Did you wait *long?*

Answer: Yes.

Reason: *Long* modifies the verb *did wait*. A word that modifies a verb is an adverb. Therefore, in sentence 1, *long* is an *adverb*.

Question 2:   Is *long* an adverb in the following sentence?

2. They are going on a *long* trip.

Answer: No.

Reason: *Long* modifies the noun *trip*. A word that modifies a noun is an *adjective*. Therefore, *long,* in sentence 2, is an *adjective*.

EXERCISE 2.   Indicate whether the italicized word is an adverb or an adjective, and tell what it modifies.

Samples:

The clock is *fast*.   *Fast* is an ___adjective___

modifying the ___N.___   ___clock___ .

She runs *fast*.   *Fast* is an ___adverb___

modifying the ___V.___   ___runs___ .

1. These shoes are *tight*.   *Tight* is an _____

modifying the _____   _____ .

2. You closed the lid *tight*.   *Tight* is an _____

modifying the _____   _____ .

3. The patient is *well*.   *Well* is an _____

modifying the _____   _____ .

4. They sang *well*.   *Well* is an _____

modifying the _____   _____ .

5. Jack works *hard*.   *Hard* is an _____

modifying the _____   _____ .

6. He is a *hard* worker.   *Hard* is an _____

modifying the _____   _____ .

7. We applied *late*.   *Late* is an _____

modifying the _____   _____ .

8. Our applications were *late*.   *Late* is an _____

modifying the _____   _____ .

9. You threw *high*.   *High* is an _____

modifying the _____   _____ .

10. Your throw was too *high*.   *High* is an _____

modifying the _____   _____ .

Summary: **Do not jump to the conclusion that a word is an adverb because it ends in *ly*, or that a word is not an adverb because it does not end in *ly*.**

To tell whether a word is an adverb, or an adjective, or any other part of speech, look at the way the word is used in its sentence.

Lesson 13 Review of Adjectives and Adverbs

Read the following passage:

Kino, a young Mexican diver, finds a beautiful rare pearl. It is very large. Immediately, word spreads in the village that he will be rich. But when Kino tries to sell the pearl, the dishonest buyers tell him it is worthless. They offer him a ridiculous price. Kino refuses to sell.

Then, murderous thieves fall upon Kino, in broad daylight as well as at night. They fail to get the pearl. Kino kills one attacker. Others, however, burn Kino's poor hut to the ground.

Kino decides to go to Mexico City, the distant capital, to try to sell the pearl. On a dark and windy night, with brave wife Juana and infant son Coyotito, he sets out on the long, dangerous journey.

They have not walked many miles, when, in the dim distance, Kino detects three approaching figures: a man on horseback and two trackers on foot. Across the saddle, a long metal object gleams in the sun. It is a rifle.

For the full story of Kino, Juana, and Coyotito, read *The Pearl*, a fascinating short novel by John Steinbeck.

EXERCISE 1.   There are thirty adjectives in the passage you have just read, not counting *a, an,* and *the*. List these adjectives in the order in which they occur, and indicate the words they modify. The first five answers have been filled in as samples.

ADJECTIVE	WORD MODIFIED
1. *young*	*diver*
2. *Mexican*	*diver*
3. *beautiful*	*pearl*
4. *rare*	*pearl*
5. *large*	*It*
6.	
7.	

ADJECTIVE	WORD MODIFIED
8. _____	_____
9. _____	_____
10. _____	_____
11. _____	_____
12. _____	_____
13. _____	_____
14. _____	_____
15. _____	_____
16. _____	_____
17. _____	_____
18. _____	_____
19. _____	_____
20. _____	_____
21. _____	_____
22. _____	_____
23. _____	_____
24. _____	_____
25. _____	_____
26. _____	_____
27. _____	_____
28. _____	_____
29. _____	_____
30. _____	_____

PARTS OF SPEECH

Read the following:

Lemuel Gulliver often went to sea as a ship's surgeon. He was ship-wrecked once in an extremely violent South Sea storm in 1699, and very nearly lost his life, but managed somehow to swim ashore. The land he had come to was not inhabited—at least it seemed so.

For nine hours Gulliver slept soundly on the beach. Awaking, he was greatly surprised to find that he could not move, for he had been firmly tied to the ground by hundreds of very thin strings. He could look only upward. The sun was unbearably hot.

Soon Gulliver felt something moving on his left leg. It advanced gently toward his chin. Curious, Gulliver bent his eyes downward and saw that it was a six-inch human, armed with bow and arrow, and followed by about forty similar creatures. So loud did Gulliver roar in astonishment that they ran back instantly. Afterward Gulliver learned that some had injured themselves seriously as they leaped desperately from his body to the ground.

Gulliver is the main character in *Gulliver's Travels*, a timelessly classic novel by Jonathan Swift.

EXERCISE 2. Altogether there are twenty-nine adverbs in the above passage. Adverbs 1–5 and the words they modify are shown as samples. List the remaining twenty-four adverbs and the words they modify, including the part of speech of the words modified.

FIRST PARAGRAPH (9 ADVERBS)

ADVERB	WORD(S) MODIFIED
1. *often*	V. *went*
2. *once*	V. *was shipwrecked*
3. *extremely*	ADJ. *violent*
4. *very*	ADV. *nearly*
5. *nearly*	V. *lost*
6. _____	_____
7. _____	_____
8. _____	_____
9. _____	_____

SECOND PARAGRAPH (8 ADVERBS)

ADVERB	WORD(S) MODIFIED
10. _____	_____
11. _____	_____
12. _____	_____
13. _____	_____
14. _____	_____
15. _____	_____
16. _____	_____
17. _____	_____

THIRD PARAGRAPH (11 ADVERBS)

ADVERB	WORD(S) MODIFIED
18. _____	_____
19. _____	_____
20. _____	_____
21. _____	_____
22. _____	_____
23. _____	_____
24. _____	_____
25. _____	_____
26. _____	_____
27. _____	_____
28. _____	_____

LAST PARAGRAPH (1 ADVERB)

ADVERB	WORD(S) MODIFIED
29. _____	_____

PARTS OF SPEECH

EXERCISE 3. Answer the following questions by writing *adverb* or *adjective* in the space provided.

What do we need to modify

1. a verb?   An _____.

2. a noun?   An _____.

3. an adjective?   An _____.

4. a pronoun?   An _____.

5. an adverb?   An _____.

EXERCISE 4. Fill in the blank with the correct choice.

Sample:

Copy the assignment __*accurately*_____ . (*accurate, accurately*)

1. You should take your work _____ . (*serious, seriously*)

2. It is _____ cold outside. (*terrible, terribly*)

3. Ripe melon tastes _____ . (*delicious, deliciously*)

4. They were _____ sorry. (*real, really*)

5. Angela behaved very _____ . (*rude, rudely*)

6. Reuben has an _____ bad cold. (*unbelievable, unbelievably*)

7. The fire spread _____ quickly. (*awful, awfully*)

8. Rush-hour traffic was _____ slow. (*painful, painfully*)

9. No one plans so _____ as Katy. (*careful, carefully*)

10. You sounded _____ yesterday. (*hoarse, hoarsely*)

Lesson 14 Prepositions

 A *preposition* relates a noun or pronoun to some other part of the sentence.

Here are some examples of what prepositions do:

1. The group *will meet **before** lunch.*
      V.   PREP.   N.

   (The preposition *before* relates the noun *lunch* to the verb *will meet*.)

2. A *letter* ***for*** *you* came today.
      N.   PREP.   PRON.

   (The preposition *for* relates the pronoun *you* to the noun *letter*.)

3. It is *cool* ***in*** the *shade.*
      ADJ.   PREP.   N.

   (The preposition *in* relates the noun *shade* to the adjective *cool*.)

4. The shelf was finished *poorly **along** the edges.*
                          ADV.   PREP.   N.

   (The preposition *along* relates the noun *edges* to the adverb *poorly*.)

By the way, a few prepositions consist of more than one word: *because of*, *in spite of*, etc.

5. We were *late **because of** the fog.*
          ADJ.   PREP.   N.

   (The preposition *because of* relates the noun *fog* to the adjective *late*.)

Caution: Do not confuse a preposition with an adverb. Compare *before* in the following pair of sentences:

1. We *met **before.***
      V.   ADV.

   (*Before* is an *adverb* modifying the verb *met*.)

2. They *met **before** lunch*.
           V.   PREP.   N.

(*Before* is a *preposition* relating the noun *lunch* to the verb *met*.)

To discover whether a word is a preposition, or an adverb, or any other part of speech, see how it is used in its sentence.

Common Prepositions

Here is a list of words commonly used as prepositions.

(If you see one of the words below in a sentence, check whether it is in fact being used as a preposition before concluding that it is one. See again sentences 1 and 2, above.)

about	by	out of
above	despite	outside
across	down	over
after	during	past
against	except	since
along	for	through
among	from	throughout
around	in	till
at	inside	to
because of	in spite of	toward
before	instead of	under
behind	into	until
below	like	up
beside	of	upon
between	off	with
beyond	on	within
but (meaning "except")		without

EXERCISE 1.　Each of the following sayings may or may not contain a preposition. If it contains a preposition, write that preposition in the space provided. If it does not, write *no prep.*

Samples:

Do not put all your eggs in one basket.　　　　　*in* _____

The early bird catches the worm.　　　　　　　*no prep.* _____

1. A word to the wise is sufficient. _____

2. Do not judge a book by its cover. _____

3. Fools and their money are soon parted. _____

4. An apple never falls far from the tree. _____

5. Birds of a feather flock together. _____

6. A house divided against itself cannot stand. _____

7. Better late than never. _____

8. People who live in glass houses should not throw stones. _____

9. Do not put off until tomorrow what you can do today. _____

10. Necessity is the mother of invention. _____

EXERCISE 2.   Change each sentence to a sentence that has the opposite meaning—and do this by changing just one word, the *preposition*, to another preposition.

Sample:

The customer wanted coffee *with* cream.

The customer wanted coffee ___*without*___ cream.

1. We waited *outside* the library.

   We waited _____ the library.

2. Take one tablet *before* each meal.

   Take one tablet _____ each meal.

3. Did someone run *into* the house?

   Did someone run _____ the house?

4. The trip *to* school took an hour.

   The trip _____ school took an hour.

5. Most of the fans were *against* us.

   Most of the fans were _____ us.

You have probably noticed by now that every preposition is followed by a noun or a pronoun.

He slammed the ball ***out of*** the ***infield.***
                             PREP.   N.

Please do not leave ***without us.***
                       PREP.   PRON.

We now turn our attention to the noun or pronoun that follows a preposition.

Object of the Preposition

The noun or pronoun that follows a preposition is the *object of the preposition.*

He slammed the ball *out of* the ***infield.***
                             PREP.   OBJ. OF PREP.

(The noun *infield* is the object of the preposition *out of.*)

Please do not leave *without **us.***
                       PREP.   OBJ. OF PREP.

(The pronoun *us* is the object of the preposition *without.*)

EXERCISE 3.   Find the *preposition* and the *object of the preposition.*

Samples:

	PREP.	OBJ. OF PREP.
Who was behind the wheel?	*behind*	*wheel*
Because of you, we could not go.	*Because of*	*you*

1. The story is about a teen. _____ _____

2. Get out of this house! _____ _____

3. Meet me outside the library. _____ _____

4. She has been sick since Friday. _____ _____

5. Wait until next week. _____ _____

6. Do you want rye bread instead of a roll? _____ _____

7. Everyone agreed except Ryan. _____ _____

8. Drop the rental DVD in the nearest return slot. _____ _____

9. Football play continued in spite of the snow.

   PREP. _____   OBJ. OF PREP. _____

10. I have never seen anything like it.

   _____   _____

Prepositional Phrases

Every day we encounter hundreds of prepositional phrases. Suppose you lost a wristwatch—almost every one of us has done something like that—and you looked for it

> *in your pockets,*
> *on the dresser,*
> *under the sofa,*
> *between the cushions,*

and, finally,

> *on your wrist,*

where you discovered it was all along.

All of the italicized expressions above, which describe locations, are *prepositional phrases.*

What Is a Prepositional Phrase?

A *prepositional phrase* is a group of words that (1) begins with a *preposition* and (2) ends with the *object of the preposition* (a noun or pronoun).

EXAMPLE OF A PREPOSITIONAL PHRASE ENDING WITH A NOUN:

I wrote **with a pen.**
  PREP. PHR.

(The prepositional phrase *with a pen* begins with the preposition *with* and ends with the noun *pen.* The noun *pen* is the object of the preposition *with.*)

A word that modifies the object of the preposition is considered part of the prepositional phrase:

I wrote **with a new pen.**
  PREP. PHR.

(The adjective *new* modifies the noun *pen* and is a part of the prepositional phrase.)

EXAMPLE OF A PREPOSITIONAL PHRASE ENDING WITH A PRONOUN:

Without her, they would have lost the game.
  PREP. PHR.

(The prepositional phrase _Without her_ consists of the preposition _without_ and the pronoun _her_. The pronoun _her_ is the object of the preposition _without_.)

EXERCISE 1.   Underline the prepositional phrase. Then, in the spaces at the right, enter the _preposition_ and the _object of the preposition._

Sample:

	PREP.	OBJ. OF PREP.
I bought a ticket for the first performance.	_for_	_performance_

1. With your help we cannot fail.

2. The Jacksons live above us.

3. Take the train instead of the bus.

4. Nate swims like a fish.

5. In spite of her failure, she will try again.

Composition Hint

Sometimes we can express an idea through either an adverb or a prepositional phrase.

Handle the glassware **_carefully_**.
  ADV.

Handle the glassware **_with care_**.
  PREP. PHR.

If you know more than one way to express your ideas, you will be a better writer.

EXERCISE 2.   Replace the italicized adverb with a prepositional phrase.

Samples:

He acted _selfishly._	_in a selfish manner_
Luckily, the bus was waiting.	_By luck_
You cannot stay _here._	_in this place_

1. Does the motor run *quietly?* _____

2. It happened *accidentally.* _____

3. Who lives *there?* _____

4. She replied *angrily.* _____

5. We worry *always.* _____

6. The child slept *restlessly.* _____

7. You are *doubtlessly* right. _____

8. Few of us face danger *fearlessly.* _____

9. The meetings are conducted *democratically.* _____

10. *Instantly,* the fire was extinguished. _____

Another Composition Hint _____

Sometimes we can express an idea through either an adjective or a prepositional phrase.

An unsigned check is ***valueless*.**
ADJ.

An unsigned check is ***of no value*.**
PREP. PHR.

EXERCISE 3. Rewrite the sentence, replacing the italicized adjective with a prepositional phrase.

Samples:

You may find yourself *penniless.*

You may find yourself without a penny.

A mayor is an *important* person.

A mayor is a person of importance.

1. Many *European* tourists visit the United States each year.

_____

2. My help was *useless*.

   _____

3. Many cars are designed to use *unleaded* gasoline.

   _____

4. The *Canadian* people are our neighbors.

   _____

5. Take the *end* seat.

   _____

EXERCISE 4.   One of the most admired short poems in American literature is "Fog," by Carl Sandburg.

> The fog comes
> on little cat feet.
>
> It sits looking
> over harbor and city
> on silent haunches
> and then moves on.

1. In which prepositional phrase does Carl Sandburg tell

   (*a*) how the fog comes? _____ _____ _____ _____

   (*b*) how the fog sits? _____ _____ _____ _____

   (*c*) where the fog looks? _____ _____ _____ _____

2. What part of speech is the
   last word of the poem? _____

Lesson 15 Conjunctions

 A *conjunction* is a word that connects other words or groups of words.

The most common conjunctions are **and, but,** and **or.**

What Kinds of Work Do Conjunctions Do?

1. **A conjunction connects *nouns:***

    *Milk **and** cheese* are dairy products.
    N.   CONJ. N.

    (The conjunction *and* connects the nouns *milk* and *cheese.*)

    *Jennifer, Joe, **or** Jamal* will lead the discussion.
    N.   N.   CONJ.   N.

    (The conjunction *or* connects the nouns *Jennifer, Joe,* and *Jamal.*)

2. **A conjunction connects *adjectives*:**

    The winners were *tired **but** happy.*
                         ADJ. CONJ. ADJ.

    (The conjunction *but* connects the adjectives *tired* and *happy.*)

3. **A conjunction connects *verbs:***

    I do not care if I *win **or** lose.*
                          V. CONJ. V.

    (The conjunction *or* connects the verbs *win* and *lose.*)

4. **A conjunction connects *pronouns*, or a *noun and a pronoun:***

    *You **and** she* are always on time.
    PRON. CONJ. PRON.

    (The conjunction *and* connects the pronouns *You* and *she.*)

    *Alex **and** I* are neighbors.
    N.   CONJ. PRON.

    (The conjunction *and* connects the noun *Alex* and the pronoun *I.*)

5. A conjunction connects *adverbs:*

It rained *gently* **but** *steadily.*
       ADV.   CONJ. ADV.

(The conjunction *but* connects the adverbs *gently* and *steadily.*)

6. A conjunction connects *prepositional phrases:*

Park *on Washington Street* **or** *on the driveway.*
     PREP. PHR.   CONJ.   PREP. PHR.

(The conjunction *or* connects the prepositional phrases *on Washington Street* and *on the driveway.*)

In addition to the above, conjunctions can make still other connections, as we shall see later.

EXERCISE 1. Find the conjunction and explain what it connects.

Sample:

You are improving slowly but surely.

The conjunction _____*but*_____ connects the _____*adverbs*_____
_____*slowly*_____ and _____*surely*_____ .

1. We were warm and comfortable.

   The conjunction _____ connects the _____
   _____ and _____ .

2. The meal was delicious but cheap.

   The conjunction _____ connects the _____
   _____ and _____ .

3. Jim called at noon and in the evening.

   The conjunction _____ connects the _____
   _____ and _____ .

4. The manager politely but firmly asked us to leave.

   The conjunction _____ connects the _____
   _____ and _____ .

5. Prices may go up or down.

   The conjunction _____ connects the _____
   _____ and _____ .

The conjunctions ***and, or,*** and ***but*** connect words or expressions of equal rank: two nouns, two adjectives, two adverbs, two prepositional phrases, etc.

POOR: They worked *quickly* and *with care.*
(The words connected are not of equal rank: *quickly* is an adverb, and *with care* is a prepositional phrase.)

BETTER: They worked *quickly* and *carefully.*
(The words connected are of equal rank: *quickly* and *carefully* are adverbs.)

However, as we have seen on page 102, a conjunction can connect a noun and a pronoun.

CORRECT: *Mary* and *I* will help.
          N.   PRON.

Whenever you write, watch your use of the conjunctions ***and, or,*** and ***but;*** make sure they connect words or expressions of equal rank.

EXERCISE 2.   Rewrite the sentence if the words connected by the conjunction are not of the same rank. If they are of the same rank, write "correct."

Samples:

Donna was tired and in an angry mood.

   Donna was tired and angry.

My neighbor and I are sports fans.

   Correct

1. We were treated decently and with fairness.

2. The problem has been discussed frequently and in a thorough manner.

3. The ball bounced off the fence and into the bushes.

4. Was the play successful or a failure?

5. I am sure they thought I was a fool and unwise.

_____

6. Tomorrow will be sunny but windy.

_____

7. The guest speaker spoke briefly but with effectiveness.

_____

8. Your brother or you must have left the door open.

_____

9. Did Alyssa's improvement in school happen suddenly or in a gradual manner?

_____

10. Their team's struggle this season seemed endless and without hope.

_____

Combining Simple Sentences

Another use for the conjunctions **and, but,** and **or** is to combine *simple sentences* into *compound sentences*. Read more about compound sentences on page 151 of Part Three.

A *simple sentence* has only one subject and one verb.

> *Paul scraped* the dishes. *I loaded* them into the dishwasher.   (*simple*
> S.   V.   S.   V.   *sentences*)

A *compound sentence* consists of two or more simple sentences joined by *and, but,* or *or.*

> *Paul scraped the dishes*, *and I loaded them into the dishwasher.* (*compound*
>   simple sentence   CONJ.   simple sentence   *sentence*)

Punctuation: A comma [,] usually precedes the conjunction.

Use the conjunction **but** to combine simple sentences that contrast with each other.

> The *boat overturned. Nobody was* injured.   (*simple sentences*)
>   S.   V.   S.   V.

> *The boat overturned*, but *nobody was injured.*   (*compound sentence*)
>   simple sentence   CONJ.   simple sentence

Use the conjunction *or* to combine simple sentences expressing a choice between two or more possibilities.

I will bring my basketball. **We** **can use** yours.   (*simple sentences*)
S.   V.   S.   V.

I will bring my basketball, *or*   **we can use yours.**   (*compound sentence*)
        simple sentence   CONJ.   simple sentence

EXERCISE 3. Using *and, but,* or *or,* combine each pair of simple sentences into a compound sentence.

Samples:

We took along warm clothing. It was not needed.

   We took along warm clothing, but it was not needed.

The weather was fine. We had a good time.

   The weather was fine, and we had a good time.

Is cash required? Is a check acceptable?

   Is cash required, or is a check acceptable?

1. Clouds covered the sky. Raindrops began to fall.

   _____

   _____

2. The engine needs a tuneup. The brakes have to be checked.

   _____

   _____

3. We called Steven. He was not at home.

   _____

4. Are you happy with the computer game? Do you want me to return it?

   _____

   _____

5. Brandon offered me his notes. I did not take them.

   _____

   _____

6. Rhonda is running for president. I am her campaign manager.

   _____

   _____

7. Ted wrote to Jenna. She did not answer.

   _____

   _____

8. Amy shut off the water. The house would have been flooded.

   _____

   _____

9. Alex apologized to me. We shook hands.

   _____

10. I warned you. You did not listen.

    _____

Lesson 16 Interjections

 An *interjection* is a word or short expression that shows sudden strong feeling.

> *Oh!* The toast is burning!
> INTERJ.

> *Oops!* I nearly fell.
> INTERJ.

> *Too bad!* Look what happened!
> INTERJ.

An interjection is considered a unit in itself and is not tied grammatically to any other word in the sentence. *Oh!* in the first example is like a sentence by itself. The same is true of *Oops!* and *Too bad!*

An interjection is usually followed by an *exclamation point* [!]. However, if the interjection is a mild one, it is followed by a *comma* [,]; the comma separates it from the rest of the sentence.

> *Oh,* excuse me.
> INTERJ.

An exclamatory sentence often follows an interjection.

> *Too bad!* Look what happened!
> INTERJ.   exclamatory sentence

EXERCISE 1. What would you say in each of the following situations? Choose your answer from the suggested replies at the end of the exercise, and write it in the space provided.

Sample:

Your coach announces that the team is getting new uniforms.

Wow! That's great!

---

1. You mop the sweat from your face with a handkerchief.

   _____

2. Someone knocks. Opening the door, you are mildly disgusted to find it is a person who has been pestering you.

   _____

3. Arriving at the pool, you find that you have left some essential equipment at home.

   _____

4. Someone accidentally steps on your painful toe.

   _____

5. You see a $12.99 price tag on a bicycle. The dealer explains it is an error.

   _____

Suggested Replies

Oh, no! I forgot my swimsuit.   Ouch! That hurts!

Oh, it's you again.   Well! You got here at last!

Man! It's hot in here!   Aha, I thought so.

EXERCISE 2.   What part of speech is the italicized word?

Reminder: To determine what part of speech a word is, check to see how that word is used in its sentence.

Samples:

A *man* answered the telephone.   _noun_____

Man the oars.   _verb_____

Man! Was I angry!   _interjection_____

1. *Fire!* Everybody out!   _____

2. Can the manager *fire* you for no reason?   _____

3. The *fire* was brought under control.   _____

4. Pollution is a *great* problem.   _____

5. *Great!* I'll be there in a minute. _____

6. The *well* ran dry.   _____

INTERJECTIONS   **109**

7. *Well*, are we ready? _____

8. Greg swims *well*. _____

9. Did you ever hear such *nonsense?* _____

10. *Nonsense!* You're all wrong. _____

Lesson 17 Review of Prepositions, Conjunctions, and Interjections

Recall that **prepositions** relate nouns or pronouns to some other part of the sentence. **Conjunctions** are words that connect other words or groups of words. **Interjections** are words or short expressions that show sudden strong feeling.

EXERCISE 1. In the following sentences, underline the prepositional phrase. Then, in the spaces at the right, enter the **preposition** and the **object of the preposition**.

Sample:

	PREP.	OBJ. OF PREP.
A road runs <u>along the river</u>.	*along*	*the river*
1. Meet me at the bus stop.		
2. A remark by that new student hurt me very much.		
3. A file on the computer desktop disappeared.		
4. No one knew the answer but William.		
5. Who was that guy sitting next to you?		
6. He met the difficult situation with courage.		
7. What did she receive from her mother?		
8. There's a party after the game.		
9. Inside her backpack were a lot of old papers.		
10. Everyone is excused except Pemba and you.		

EXERCISE 2. Use *and,* *but,* or *or* to combine each pair of sentences into one compound sentence.

Sample:

I played the CD at top volume. My mother told me to turn it down.

I played the CD at top volume, and my mother told me to turn it down.

1. You are taking chemistry this year. Mariel is taking physics this year.

_____

2. Does the DVD player work all right? Do you want a refund?

_____

3. We called Raj at 11 o'clock. He did not answer.

_____

4. All of a sudden, lightning flashed. Thunder rolled.

_____

5. I am bringing nachos and salsa to the class party. You are bringing pretzels and potato chips.

_____

6. You and Josh may be going on the trip. I have other things to do.

_____

7. Kayla believed her poem was good. Her parents, best friend, and English teacher thought she should enter it in a competition.

_____

_____

8. For Thanksgiving, you are going to your grandparents. I am staying home.

_____

9. Is this movie all right with you? Do you want to see a different one?

_____

10. Sakito thinks he is the smartest person in the class. Others don't think so.

_____

EXERCISE 3. Add an interjection to each of the following sentences, in keeping with the mood suggested in the parentheses following the sentence.

Sample:

You scored 1300 on your SATs. (approval)

Great! You scored 1300 on your SATs.

1. It's time to go already. (disappointment)

2. Did he fumble the football again? (exasperation)

3. You got here in one piece. (relief)

4. I won the statewide creative writing award! (excitement)

5. The doors are locked and we can't get out. (fear)

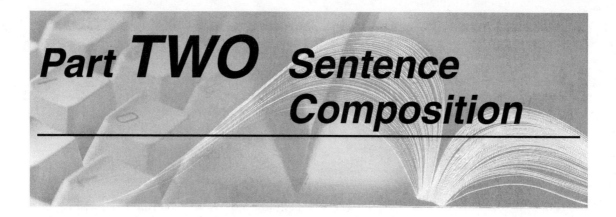

Part *TWO* *Sentence Composition*

All writing begins with the sentence. In Part One, we explored the parts of speech, the building blocks of sentences. This part directs attention to the structure and quality of sentences. It asks you to judge between good and bad examples—and encourages you to write good ones. With a little practice, you can produce sentences that say what you mean in a fresh and effective way.

Lesson 18 Characteristics of Good Sentences

Sentences vary widely in style and subject matter. Yet all good sentences have certain qualities in common.

1. Good sentences do not waste words. They use only enough words to carry the thought. Nor do they wander. They make their point . . . and stop (pages 123–126).

WORDY: The difficulties we cause in this all-too-brief life of ours are often those that we bring upon ourselves, even if unintentionally.

CONCISE: Most of the shadows of this life are caused by our standing in our own sunshine. (Ralph Waldo Emerson)

2. Good sentences are clear. They express a thought precisely and directly (pages 126–132).

MUDDLED: Andrew got up to bat and sent it into the right-field stands.

CLEAR: Andrew got up to bat and sent the ball into the right-field stands.

3. Good sentences have unity. They stick to one general topic in a sentence (pages 145–148).

LACKING IN UNITY: Good tennis players don't have to work very hard, but golfers sometimes seem to enjoy the game more.

UNIFIED: A good tennis player works hard but never looks as though he is.

4. Good sentences are coherent, using accurate connectives (page 127).

LACKING COHERENCE: Because Sue was our best pitcher, she didn't get a chance to pitch in the playoffs.

COHERENT: Although Sue was our best pitcher, she didn't get a chance to pitch in the playoffs.

5. Good sentences are varied in structure. They do not always follow a set pattern (pages 132–145).

> MONOTONOUS: Isabella is pretty and rich. She is also a fabulous singer. I envy her.

> VARIED: Isabella is not only pretty and rich but also a fabulous singer. How I envy her!

6. Good sentences call upon strong, specific nouns and vivid verbs to convey the thought. They use adjectives and adverbs sparingly but effectively (pages 124–126).

> DULL: The duck landed on the ice unsuccessfully and finally came to a stop after a long slide along the ice on the pond.

> VIVID: The mallard landed uncertainly on the ice, skidded and flopped along for twenty feet, and then scrambled to its feet with dignity.

7. Good sentences are pleasing to read, usually an enjoyable part of a larger whole (pages 150–155).

8. Good sentences are complete, neither fragments (pages 155–164) nor run-ons (pages 164–168).

9. Good sentences are technically correct, following accepted standards of usage (pages 149–230) and spelling (pages 221–230).

Comparing Sentences

It is helpful to read good sentences written by others. Here is an example of a powerful, simple sentence:

> *At the center of nonviolence stands the principle of love.* (Martin Luther King, Jr.)

How much less effective it would have been if stated in this way:

> *People who believe in nonviolence and practice it are really showing that they love others.*

Question: Why is the first sentence so much better?

Answer: The first sentence is direct, clear, concise.

EXERCISE 1.   Which sentence in each pair do you consider better? Tell why.

1. *a.* We went on the roller coaster and then we went on the haunted house ride and then we went on the monorail.

   b. We went on the roller coaster, the haunted house ride, and the monorail.

   _____

   _____

2. *a.* At the library, I picked up a Harry Potter book and a book about photography.

   b. I went to the library and I picked up a book about Harry Potter and a book that tells all about photography.

   _____

   _____

3. *a.* The family had all agreed on a camping spot for our vacation, and Brad suddenly disagreed.

   b. The family had all agreed on a camping spot for our vacation, but Brad suddenly disagreed.

   _____

   _____

4. *a.* I ordered a sandwich made with cheese, a bag filled with potato chips, and an apple for lunch.

   b. For lunch, I ordered a cheese sandwich, a bag of potato chips, and an apple.

   _____

   _____

5. *a.* Liv had accepted Joel's invitation to the dance, and she changed her mind with no explanation.

   b. Liv had accepted Joel's invitation to the dance, but she changed her mind with no explanation.

   _____

   _____

Completing Comparisons

In the previous section, we compared sentences to see which ones were better. We can also use comparison as a writing tool to make sentences more concise, lively, and enjoyable to read.

Consider the following sentence, in which baseball players are compared to bees:

The baseball players gathered around the umpire like angry bees.

By using the image of the angry bees, we do not have to say that the players were aggressive and quick in their movements or that their complaints sounded like a loud buzz around the umpire. The image of the bees does that for us. Using a comparison in this way saves words and creates interest.

If you paid close attention to your speech, you would find that you use many comparisons. Some are *direct*, with *like* or *as*: "as strong as an ox," "as timid as a mouse," "like a lion." Others are *indirect*: "Joan was a tiger on the field." (Joan played as savagely as a tiger.) Both forms are a kind of poetry. Direct comparisons are called *similes*. Indirect ones are *metaphors*. In the following exercise, try your skill in writing sentences with comparisons.

EXERCISE 2.   Complete each of the following with an original comparison.

Sample:

A book is like *a new friend waiting to meet you.*

1. A thunderstorm is like _____

2. A cat is like _____

3. A final exam is like _____

4. A forest fire is like _____

5. Playing basketball is like _____

6. The school cafeteria is like _____

7. A good friend is like _____

8. The city at night is like _____

9. Browsing the Web is like _____

10. Swimming in the ocean is like _____

Writing Sentences

When you begin to write a sentence, you should know where you are going with it. Complete the thought you set out to express. As you put your thought in writing, remember the nine characteristics of good sentences, outlined at the beginning of this lesson. Lesson 19 will show some specific ways to write effective sentences.

EXERCISE 3.   Complete each of the following to make a good sentence.

Sample:

My final grades *improved so much over last year's that my scholarship chances rose dramatically.*

1. My major ambition in life is to _____

2. After dinner, I am planning _____

3 My favorite way to spend Saturday is to _____

4. Last summer, I _____

5. Computers _____

6. For dessert _____

7. When the football game was over _____

8. I hope _____

9. At the end of the movie _____

10. Why didn't _____

EXERCISE 4.   Write a single good sentence that tells about each of the following.

Sample:

a favorite pet

I once had a parakeet named Humphrey, who enjoyed flying around the room.

1. an unusual coincidence that occurred recently

_____

2. a happy moment in your life

_____

3. something you are proud of

_____

4. a surprise

_____

5. the person who influences you most

_____

Revising Sentences

Revising is an important part of the writing process. It is helpful to reread what you have written. Chances are, you will discover an error, uncover something that may not be clear to readers, or simply find a more interesting or memorable way to say what you wrote. Are your sentences technically correct, precise, concise, and effective? Make it a habit to answer this question by rereading and revising every sentence before you send it out into the world.

EXERCISE 5.   Select ten of the fifteen sentences you wrote for Exercises 3 and 4 and revise them. Aim for conciseness and clarity by eliminating unnecessary or vague words.

Sample:

Original sentence: My final grades improved so much over last year's that my scholarship chances rose dramatically.

Revised sentence: My scholarship chances skyrocketed because my final grades greatly improved this year.

1. _____

_____

2. _____

_____

3. _____

_____

4. _____

_____

5. _____

_____

6. _____

_____

7. _____

_____

8. _____

_____

9. _____

_____

10. _____

_____

Lesson 19 Clear, Forceful Sentences

Question: What makes writing "good"?

Answer: Good writing has four major characteristics: conciseness (economy), clarity, variety, and unity.

Conciseness (Economy)

Never make a thought more complicated than it really is. Express yourself as simply and directly as possible. Here are some errors to avoid.

Useless Words

Eliminate all useless words.

> WORDY: At the soccer match, Joel met up with two friends from elementary school.

> CONCISE: At the soccer match, Joel met two friends from elementary school. (Eliminate *up with*.)

Duplication

Avoid saying the same thing twice, even though in different words.

> WORDY: We flew by air to Cleveland and returned back by bus.

> CONCISE: We flew to Cleveland and returned by bus. (Eliminate *by air* and *back*.)

Wordy Construction

Do not use too many words to express an idea. Condense a phrase (see pages 137–140, 145) to a word, a clause to a phrase or even a word. Be a *which* hunter and eliminate all unnecessary *which*es (or *that*s).

> WORDY: The newscast which was televised this morning on a local station described a suspicious car that had a license plate from the state of North Dakota.

> CONCISE: This morning's local television newscast described a suspicious car with a North Dakota license plate.

Pretentious Language

Unless you are being humorous, do not use a longer word if a simpler one will do the job. Save the longer word for a context in which the simpler one does not work.

> PRETENTIOUS: The feline member of our family loves to frolic, gambol, and cavort for considerable periods of time with the canine member of our family menage.

> SIMPLER: Our cat often plays with the family dog.

Note: The first sentence might be acceptable in a humorous essay that mocks pretension.

Piled-up Modifiers

Avoid piling adjective upon adjective, adverb upon adverb. Where possible, use specific nouns and verbs to reduce the number of modifiers.

> WORDY: The young, immature baby of but a year walked unsteadily and shakily across the floor into the outstretched, waiting arms of her waiting mother.

> CONCISE: The one-year-old tottered across the floor into her mother's outstretched arms.

EXERCISE 1.   In each pair of sentences, choose the more concise and point out why the chosen sentence is preferable.

1. *a.* The house which stood on the corner of Main Street and Maple Avenue has been declared a landmark with historic associations.

   b. The house on the corner of Main Street and Maple Avenue has been declared a historic landmark.

   _____

   _____

2. *a.* July daytime temperatures this year have averaged about 73 degrees.

   b. July temperatures during the day this year have averaged about 73 degrees on the average.

   _____

   _____

3. *a.* The Paso Fino is a relatively small horse with a distinctive, appealing gait.

   b. Of the equine breed, the Paso Fino is a horse that is relatively small but with a gait that is as distinctive as it is appealing.

   _____

   _____

4. *a.* The Chrono watch is cheap in price but efficient in use.

   b. The Chrono watch is cheap but efficient.

   _____

   _____

5. *a.* When Sasha found she had lost her keys, she rushed to the store she had just left.

   b. When Sasha found she had carelessly and thoughtlessly lost her keys, she rushed rapidly and swiftly into the store she had just left.

   _____

   _____

EXERCISE 2.　　Rewrite the following selections to make them more concise. Keep in mind the preceding suggestions.

1. The bus that I take to school seems to have one shock absorber that is faulty.

   _____

   _____

2. My favorite pet among all pets is the canine pet.

   _____

   _____

3. My brother owns an old car that has rust.

   _____

   _____

4. In *Huckleberry Finn* it tells the story of a boy on the Mississippi.

   _____

   _____

5. The Biltmore House in Asheville is a magnificent house, probably the largest mansion in the nation.

   _____

   _____

6. Paint that has lead as its base should be removed from all buildings located everywhere.

   _____

   _____

7. She was a tiny little girl with a big, huge, gigantic, booming voice.

_____

_____

8. The rich ancient old man who had piles of money picked up a wad of cash with his hands.

_____

_____

9. Bill waited outside of the classroom while Scott, who was very, very late, was still inside of the classroom.

_____

_____

10. I fixed up each and every last one of my wrong mistakes before I saved the file.

_____

_____

Clarity and Specificity

Write clearly as well as concisely. Here are some errors to avoid.

Unclear Antecedents

Make certain that a pronoun has a clear antecedent (see pages 52–54 in Part One and page 196 in Part Three). Reword the sentences or supply a needed noun.

CONFUSING: Use that towel to wipe your face and put it in the clothes hamper.
(The face or the towel?)

CLEAR: Use that towel to wipe your face and put the towel in the clothes hamper.

CONFUSING: If papers are left behind by sloppy hikers, burn them.
(The papers or the hikers?)

CLEAR: Any papers left behind by sloppy hikers should be burned.

If necessary, quote the speaker's actual words to make the meaning clearer.

CONFUSING: Linda told her mother that she had left the lawn sprinklers on.
(Is the antecedent of "she" Linda or her mother?)

CLEAR: Linda told her mother, "I left the lawn sprinklers on."

CLEAR: Linda told her mother, "You left the lawn sprinklers on."

Dangling Modifiers

A modifier dangles if it is placed so that it seems to modify a word it was not intended to modify. Put a modifier close to the word it modifies. Sometimes the word itself must be supplied.

DANGLING: Turning the corner, the post office was on the left.
(The post office was not turning the corner.)

CLEAR: Turning the corner, I noticed the post office on my left.

CLEAR: As I turned the corner, I noticed the post office on my left.

CONFUSING: Tracy saw a deer riding her bike through the Hopkins meadow.
(A deer riding a bike?)

CLEAR: Riding her bike through the Hopkins meadow, Tracy saw a deer.

CONFUSING: At the age of three, Mario's mother remarried.
(At the age of three, Mario's mother could not have already had Mario, let alone be remarrying.)

CLEAR: When Mario was three, his mother remarried.

CONFUSING: While working in the library, a new shipment of books arrived.
(The books are not working; the library worker is.)

CLEAR: While I was working in the library, a new shipment of books arrived.

CONFUSING: At the party, packages were given to all the children filled with Halloween candy.
(The children may be filled later!)

CLEAR: At the party, packages filled with Halloween candy were given to all the children.

Inaccurate Connectives

Use the connective that expresses your thought accurately.

CONFUSING: I wanted to go skating, and Angela preferred hiking.

CLEAR: I wanted to go skating, but Angela preferred hiking.

CONFUSING: Because Ben was on a visit to his ill grandmother, he still got his term paper in on time.

CLEAR: Although Ben was on a visit to his ill grandmother, he still got his term paper in on time.

The Inexact Word

Be sure to choose the word that expresses your thought accurately.

CONFUSING: Our Saturday project is to install all broken windows in the school.

CLEAR: Our Saturday project is to replace all broken windows in the school.

CONFUSING: Don't fail to miss tonight's rerun of *The Simpsons*.

CLEAR: Don't miss tonight's rerun of *The Simpsons*.

CLEAR: Don't fail to see tonight's rerun of *The Simpsons*.

EXERCISE 3. In each pair of sentences, choose the clearer one and point out why the chosen sentence is preferable.

1. *a.* Listening for the train, my attention was captured by the beeping of car horns.

   b. As I was listening for the train, my attention was captured by the beeping of car horns.

   _____

   _____

2. *a.* Maria told Consuelo, "You've just won the athlete-of-the-month award."

   b. Maria told Consuelo that she had just won the athlete-of-the-month award.

   _____

   _____

3. *a.* We thought everyone had accepted Mike's suggestion, and suddenly Jason got up to object strongly.

   b. We thought everyone had accepted Mike's suggestion, but suddenly Jason got up to object strongly.

   _____

   _____

4. *a.* Regular attendance is a major cause of failure in school.

   b. Irregular attendance is a major cause of failure in school.

   _____

   _____

5. *a.* I used moist heat for my sore elbow, and it disappeared.

   b. I used moist heat for my sore elbow, and the soreness disappeared.

_____

_____

EXERCISE 4.   Rewrite the following selections to make them clearer. Keep in mind the preceding suggestions.

1. Grandma loves to watch passersby sitting in her chair on the porch.

_____

_____

2. Lam told his brother that he had been accepted at Duke University.

_____

_____

3. Because Ellen had been away for the summer vacation, she still was able to return for Miranda's birthday party.

_____

_____

4. Having misplaced my ticket, my chance of seeing the Bulls play the Lakers was slim.

_____

_____

5. The problem of driving to Craggy Gardens on the Blue Ridge Parkway was good visibility.

_____

_____

6. I enjoy seeing the city lights flying overhead in a plane.

_____

_____

7. Grab the racket and ball and then put it in the air.

_____

_____

8. Although Pamee studied carefully, she got the highest grade on the final exam.

_____

_____

CLEAR, FORCEFUL SENTENCES

9. Speaking sarcastically, the report was read by the secretary of the organization.

_____

_____

10. She cracked the eggs in the bowl in front of her cousins and beat them with a wire whip.

_____

_____

Vague, General Words

To add clarity and forcefulness to your writing, use specific words.

VAGUE:	We walked up a steep peak and rejoiced at the top.
SPECIFIC:	We clambered up the cone of Mt. Katahdin and shouted, "We made it!"
VAGUE:	On our western trip, we visited three national parks.
SPECIFIC:	On our western trip, we visited Rocky Mountain National Park, Grand Canyon, and Bryce Canyon.
VAGUE:	We had several different kinds of transportation.
SPECIFIC:	We tried horseback riding, canoeing, and helicoptering.

EXERCISE 5.   For each of the following pairs, write the word or phrase that is more specific, more concrete.

1. golden retriever, dog   _____

2. horse, thoroughbred   _____

3. sport, soccer   _____

4. daisy, flower   _____

5. reptile, rattlesnake   _____

6. tangerine, fruit   _____

7. computer, PC   _____

8. animal, cheetah   _____

9. Mars, planet   _____

10. color, ultramarine   _____

EXERCISE 6.   From the list below, select a more specific word or phrase for each italicized word or phrase in the sentences.

basketball players	*The Great Gatsby*	*Newsweek*
car	hectic	purple
City Hall	jittery	raced
English	lemon meringue pie	reading
flounder	peas	strode
football game	plunged	sycamore
gazed	poured	Thanksgiving
grandmother	*Macbeth*	waddled

1. During *a holiday*, we visited my *relative* in Seattle and went to a *game*.

   _____

   _____

2. For dinner, we had *a vegetable*, *a fish*, and a delicious *dessert*.

   _____

   _____

3. In *school*, we studied *a play*.

   _____

   _____

4. The duck *walked* along the edge of the pond and then *went* into the water.

   _____

   _____

5. That sturdy *tree* that stands near *a building* is an old one.

   _____

   _____

6. In the *motor vehicle*, we *drove quickly* to the stop light. My mother was *upset*.

   _____

   _____

7. The *athletes came* out of the plane and *went* to a waiting bus.

   _____

   _____

8. As we *looked* at the sunset, we noticed that *a color* predominated.

_____

_____

9. I enjoy *a hobby* especially when I am tired, after a *hard* day.

_____

_____

10. I went to the library and took out *a book* and *a magazine.*

_____

_____

Varying Sentences

To keep your readers interested, introduce variety into your writing. Vary both the length and the type of sentence.

Sentence Length

As we have noted, conciseness is always a desirable goal. By avoiding padding and unnecessary words, you can create a concise sentence. Concise sentences don't necessarily mean short ones, though. The following sentences use words economically but vary in length.

SHORT: Throw caution to the wind.

LONGER: If we had wings, we would soar like eagles.

STILL LONGER: Only one thing is better than winning, and that is winning fairly.

Sentence Type

For variety, use an occasional question, exclamation, or command, but don't overdo.

QUESTION: Where did I leave my tennis racket?

EXCLAMATION: I just remembered—the public courts!

COMMAND: Call the pro shop and say I'm on my way.

POLITE REQUEST: Please let my mother know I'll be late.

EXERCISE 7. Revise each of the following sentences according to the directions given in parentheses.

1. Once upon a time, in a cramped, rickety, little house with a collapsing roof, there lived a very tiny woman with springy red curls who was afraid to venture even her toe out the front door. (*Shorten; make concise.*)

_____

_____

2. Fleas jump. (*Lengthen; expand on description.*)

_____

_____

3. While classes are in session, you should close your locker door quietly. (*Make a command.*)

_____

_____

4. Sarah needs the costumes. Take them to her. (*Make a polite request.*)

_____

_____

5. There is a question about whether Sam will play quarterback in this week's game. (*Make a question.*)

_____

_____

Subject-Not-First Sentence

Avoid monotony by not beginning every sentence with the subject. When a shift in placement is both natural and effective, begin a sentence with a word other than the subject. Formations that can work well at the start of a sentence are listed below. Again, don't overdo.

ADVERB:	Wearily, the home team went onto the field for the fifteenth inning.
*ADVERB CLAUSE:	Although yellow sweet corn is more abundant in our area, Dad and I prefer the white.
*ADVERB PHRASE:	After much soul-searching, Hanaka decided to enroll in a premed course.
THERE:	There are still many undiscovered galaxies.
PREPOSITIONAL PHRASE: (See pages 142–145.)	Contrary to popular belief, a person's hair cannot turn white overnight.
PARTICIPIAL PHRASE: (See pages 142–145.)	Finding the passage blocked, the cave explorers retraced their steps.
INFINITIVE PHRASE: (See pages 142–145.)	To melt its way through spring snows, the skunk cabbage runs temperatures higher than its surroundings.
PREPOSITIONAL PHRASE WITH GERUND: (See pages 142–145.)	Before starting the car, adjust seat belts and rearview mirrors.

continued

*See Part Three for a discussion of clauses (pages 151–155) and phrases (page 156). Here we define an *adverb clause* as a group of words that contains a subject and verb and that functions as an adverb (for example, telling how or when). An *adverb phrase* also functions as an adverb, but this group of words does *not* contain a subject and verb.

CLEAR, FORCEFUL SENTENCES   133

APPOSITIVE: A language expert for the United Nations, Georges
(See page 136.)   Schmidt can translate 66 languages.

EXERCISE 8.   For each sentence below, write the word or words that have been placed before the subject for variety. Then write down what kind of formation the word or words are.

Sample:

Having the best voice, Lori won the lead role in the musical.

Having the best voice; participial phrase
_____

1. Long after his death, Herman Melville became famous as a great American writer.

_____

_____

2. Energetically, the children swung at the pinata, hoping to release the candy inside.

_____

_____

3. Although fish are natural inhabitants of the sea, they can become seasick.

_____

_____

4. Checking the car for fibers, the crime scene investigator reached for a specimen bag.

_____

_____

5. A new student, Eric was eager to make friends.

_____

_____

EXERCISE 9.   Revise each of the sentences by moving a word or words before the subject.

1. The liquid inside young coconuts can substitute for blood plasma in an emergency.

_____

_____

2. Emily Dickinson published only seven poems during her lifetime.

_____

_____

3. Florence Nightingale spent the last 50 years of her life as an invalid because she had been weakened by a fever during the Crimean War.

_____

_____

4. Serena Williams triumphantly smiled after defeating Justine Henin in the Italian Open in 2002. (two possibilities)

_____

_____

5. Barry Bonds, who plays left field for the San Francisco Giants, set the all-time major league single-season home run record in 2001, with 73 home runs. (two possibilities)

_____

_____

6. Forensics is a fascinating field of study that has attracted many new students.

_____

_____

7. Fly fishing, which requires patience and dexterity, is a challenging sport.

_____

_____

8. Dogs are intelligent and attuned to humans, so they make good working companions.

_____

_____

9. Nursing is a good career choice and is suitable for both men and women.

_____

_____

10. Soccer is a popular sport worldwide, and its popularity has increased in the United States.

_____

_____

Appositives

Use appositives to achieve conciseness and vary the sentence structure (see also Lesson 25, page 203).

> WITHOUT APPOSITIVES: The eagle, which is the U.S. national symbol, won out over the turkey, which was Benjamin Franklin's choice.
>
> WITH APPOSITIVES: The eagle, the U.S. national symbol, won out over the turkey, Benjamin Franklin's choice.
>
> WITHOUT APPOSITIVES: The medieval dinner plate was often a thick slice of stale bread and was called a trencher.
>
> WITH APPOSITIVES: The medieval dinner plate, the trencher, was often a thick slice of stale bread.

EXERCISE 10.   Point out the appositives in each of the following and tell what noun each is associated with.

1. Byron White, an All-American football player at the University of Colorado, became a Justice of the Supreme Court.

   _____

2. Copper Canyon, a huge cleft in the earth of northwestern Mexico, is the home of the Tarahumara Indians.

   _____

3. Sea otters, the acrobats of the sea, are fascinating to watch.

   _____

4. Caligula, ruthless emperor of Rome, got his name from the military boots he wore as a child.

   _____

5. George Washington Carver, pioneering plant experimenter, developed 49 different dyes from the scuppernong grape.

   _____

EXERCISE 11.   In each of the following, substitute an appositive for a clause or a sentence.

1. Napoleon Bonaparte, who was a military genius, had once been expelled from the army in disgrace.

   _____

   _____

2. Connemara is a lovely old estate in Flat Rock, North Carolina. It was once the home of the poet Carl Sandburg.

_____

_____

3. The cornea, which is an important part of the eye's structure, takes its oxygen directly from the air.

_____

_____

4. Evan McMichael, who is an optimist and a planner, is an inspiration to his friends.

_____

_____

5. Stephen King is considered a master of horror. He has written many bestsellers.

_____

_____

6. Machu Picchu was an ancient Incan city. It thrived at one time in Peru.

_____

_____

7. Marianne, who was a competitive swimmer, began training for the triathlon.

_____

_____

8. Copernicus was a Polish astronomer. He developed a theory that formed the basis of modern astronomy.

_____

_____

9. My uncle, who is an Italian count, invited me to visit his family's villa in Sicily.

_____

_____

10. Edward Jenner was an English physician. He introduced the practice of vaccination.

_____

_____

Compound Subjects and Predicates

We studied compound subjects and verbs (predicates) in Part One, pages 38 to 44. Using compound subjects or predicates can help streamline writing. The following examples show how.

When possible, combine two separate sentences into a single sentence with a compound subject.

TWO SENTENCES: Leah supported the new cafeteria regulations. The twins also supported them.

COMPOUND SUBJECT: Leah and the twins supported the new cafeteria regulations.

Another way to make your writing flow is to avoid the *and I, and we, and they* habit. For instance, read the following sentence:

They saw the laptop computer, and they borrowed it without asking permission.

You can avoid needless repetition by getting rid of the second "they":

They saw the laptop computer and borrowed it without asking permission.

Use an occasional compound predicate instead of a compound sentence or two separate sentences.

COMPOUND SENTENCE: I visited the local library and I found the latest mystery by Janet Evanovich.

COMPOUND PREDICATE: I visited the local library and found the latest mystery by Janet Evanovich.

TWO SENTENCES: *Gone with the Wind* was rejected many times. It was finally published.

COMPOUND PREDICATE: *Gone with the Wind* was rejected many times but was finally published.

EXERCISE 12.   In each of the following pairs of sentences, point out which one contains a compound subject or a compound predicate. Write the letter of your answer on the line at the left.

_____ 1. *a.* Ginnie loves Chinese egg rolls. Tammy does too.

       b. Ginnie and Tammy love Chinese egg rolls.

_____ 2. *a.* Oksana enrolled in a quilting course and expects to travel to Knoxville in July.

       b. Oksana enrolled in a quilting course, and she expects to travel to Knoxville in July.

_____ 3. *a.* The Peace Corps helps Third World nations with their problems. It also broadens the lives of the volunteers.

       b. The Peace Corps helps Third World nations with their problems and also broadens the lives of the volunteers.

_____ 4. *a.* New York police and firefighters performed heroically on September 11, 2001.

      b. New York police performed heroically on September 11, 2001. Firefighters did also.

_____ 5. *a.* Charles Babbage thought out the basic principles of modern computers. He didn't have electronic solutions for his challenges.

      b. Charles Babbage thought out the basic principles of modern computers but didn't have electronic solutions for his challenges.

EXERCISE 13.   Condense each of the following by substituting compound subjects and compound predicates for pairs of simple sentences or for compound sentences.

1. Jackie went to the Florida-Clemson game. Rebecca also went.

   _____

   _____

2. Bhavin completed the bookcase. Then he began the chest of drawers.

   _____

   _____

3. We visited the Grand Canyon and then we headed toward the Petrified Forest.

   _____

   _____

4. Bob's uncle appeared on *Jeopardy*, and he was the champion for three days.

   _____

   _____

5. In the Midwest, Notre Dame usually has a strong football team. So does Michigan.

   _____

   _____

6. I bought tickets for the rock concert Friday night. Chris did, too.

   _____

   _____

7. He stopped at the mall, and after that he went to the CD store.

   _____

   _____

8. Hurricanes often travel up the East Coast. They can cause a lot of damage.

_____

_____

9. Von studied his chemistry notes. He took the chemistry exam on Thursday.

_____

_____

10. Cara stormed into the band practice room, and she took her seat.

_____

_____

Complex Sentences

A string of simple or compound sentences can make for dull reading. Use complex sentences (page 152) to add variety and show more accurately the connection between ideas. By using complex sentences, you can avoid overusing *and*, *but*, and *so*.

SIMPLE SENTENCES:	Thomas Edison was still in possession of his sight. He found braille preferable to visual reading.
COMPLEX SENTENCE:	Though he was still in possession of his sight, Thomas Edison found braille preferable to visual reading.
COMPOUND SENTENCE:	The thin atmosphere at 12,000 feet above sea level barely supports fire, and La Paz, Bolivia, is nearly a fireproof city.
COMPLEX SENTENCE:	Because the thin atmosphere at 12,000 feet above sea level barely supports fire, La Paz, Bolivia, is nearly a fireproof city.

EXERCISE 14.   Point out the complex sentence in each of the following pairs by writing the letter of the correct choice and then writing the subordinate clause, (that is, a clause that cannot function alone as a sentence; see pages 152–153).

1. *a.* We must support efforts to save wild plants. They may yet provide cures for presently incurable diseases.

   b. Because wild plants may yet provide cures for presently incurable diseases, we must support efforts to save them.

_____

_____

2. *a.* When Jackson arrived late at the meeting, we all greeted him in stony silence.

   b. Jackson arrived late at the meeting. We all greeted him in stony silence.

   _____

   _____

3. *a.* Because the Navajo language is difficult to master, it was used as a code by the United States in World War II.

   b. The Navajo language is difficult to master, and it was used as a code by the United States in World War II.

   _____

   _____

4. *a.* Berengaria, wife of Richard the Lion-Hearted, was queen of England. She never even visited there.

   b. Although Berengaria, wife of Richard the Lion-Hearted, was queen of England, she never even visited there.

   _____

   _____

5. *a.* While Charlotte was weeding the vegetable patch, Dan was watering the large lawn.

   b. Charlotte was weeding the vegetable patch, and Dan was watering the large lawn.

   _____

   _____

EXERCISE 15.   By using proper connectives (page 127), combine each of the following into a good complex sentence.

1. Terry loses. He is always a good sport.

   _____

   _____

2. Some major artists struggled in poverty during their lifetimes. Pablo Picasso was famous and wealthy.

   _____

   _____

3. I took twelve golf lessons. Then I felt more confident on the course. (*Hint:* Use *after.*)

   _____

   _____

CLEAR, FORCEFUL SENTENCES

4. At one time, the bison population in North America was hunted mercilessly. The numbers dropped from perhaps 13 million to a few hundred.

_____

_____

5. The Eagles had been expected to lose the game. They won a smashing victory over the Giants.

_____

_____

6. Kim practiced her ice skating five hours a day. She won the regional championship.

_____

_____

7. He used his sharp mind. He was able to solve the mystery. (*Hint:* Use *by.*)

_____

_____

8. Albert Einstein formulated the theory of relativity. He won the Nobel Prize in Physics in 1921.

_____

_____

9. The state university hired a first-rate coach and recruited talented players. They lost the national championship.

_____

_____

10. She used a haircolor kit. She had red hair. (*Hint:* Use *after.*)

_____

_____

Verbals

For variety, introduce verbals (see pages 161–164 in Part Three) into your writing.

WITHOUT PARTICIPLE: I discovered an interest in various kinds of mushrooms. I decided to take a course in botany.

WITH PARTICIPLE: Having discovered an interest in various kinds of mushrooms, I decided to take a course in botany.

WITHOUT GERUND:	We all celebrated after we had won the softball championship.
WITH GERUND:	We all celebrated after winning the softball championship.
WITHOUT INFINITIVE:	Lars read *Plutarch's Lives* in order that he might learn more about the Roman emperors.
WITH INFINITIVE:	Lars read *Plutarch's Lives* to learn more about the Roman emperors.

EXERCISE 16.   In each of the following pairs of sentences, point out the verbal by writing the letter of the correct choice and then writing the verbal.

1. *a.* After gathering the suspects together, the private investigator Kinsey Millhone identified the murderer.

   b. The private investigator Kinsey Millhone gathered the suspects together and identified the murderer.

   _____

2. *a.* So that she might be sure of a ticket for the rock concert, Shelley got in line early in the morning.

   b. To be sure of a ticket for the rock concert, Shelley got in line early in the morning.

   _____

3. *a.* Having studied Spanish for three years in high school, Paul nervously asked directions in Bogotá.

   b. After he had studied Spanish for three years in high school, Paul nervously asked directions in Bogotá.

   _____

4. *a.* Before you leave the house, close all the windows.

   b. Before leaving the house, close all the windows.

   _____

5. *a.* In order that he might get a part in the school play, Doug read the play over and over.

   b. To get a part in the school play, Doug read the play over and over.

   _____

Improve these sentences by using verbals for some of the verbs.

1. Before he found the perfect filament for a light bulb, Thomas Edison unsuccessfully tried hundreds.

   _____

   _____

2. Max saved his money for months in order that he might buy a new surfboard.

   _____

   _____

3. Juan heard the score of the Rams-Lions game. He told us all at dinner.

   _____

   _____

4. Suzanne haunted flea markets in order that she might add to her collection of vintage clothing.

   _____

   _____

5. Spiders help humans. They destroy a hundred times their number in insects. (*Hint:* Use *by.*)

   _____

   _____

6. Carrie read her assignment. She realized she had not left enough time to do it.

   _____

   _____

7. So that he might win the top prize, Maurice wrote an outstanding paper.

   _____

   _____

8. Lara received a nice surprise, and she danced around the room.

   _____

   _____

9. My mom bought extra food for the party because she knows how much my friends eat.

   _____

   _____

10. She invited her friends over after she cooked a huge pot of spaghetti.

_____

_____

Unity

Be sure that every part of a sentence is related to one main idea. Correct a lack of unity by breaking a sentence into shorter sentences or by subordinating one part of a sentence to a main part. (See pages 140–142, 152, and 166–170.)

LACKING UNITY: The cockroach is a survivor, and the body can survive for weeks if the head is carefully removed.

HAVING UNITY: The cockroach is a survivor. The body can survive for weeks if the head is carefully removed.

LACKING UNITY: The ancestors of the horse were only a foot tall, and modern Percherons may stand over five feet at the shoulders.

HAVING UNITY: Although the ancestors of the horse were only a foot tall, modern Percherons may stand over five feet at the shoulders.

Overlapping Construction

Avoid a series of *that*, *which*, or *who* clauses. Too many make a sentence unwieldy.

UNWIELDY: In the 1860s, a New York firm offered a prize which would be awarded for a satisfactory substitute for ivory which was used in the manufacture of billiard balls which were in demand because of the growing popularity of billiards.

MANAGEABLE: In the 1860s, a New York firm offered a prize for an ivory substitute. Ivory had been used in the manufacture of billiard balls for the increasingly popular game of billiards.

Parallel Structure

Be sure items are parallel. Ordinarily, *and* and *but* connect like grammatical elements—for example, two or more nouns, verbs, adjectives, phrases, or clauses.

NOT PARALLEL: At camp, we most enjoyed swimming, hiking, and how to play volleyball.

PARALLEL: At camp, we most enjoyed swimming, hiking, and playing volleyball.

_____

CLEAR, FORCEFUL SENTENCES

NOT PARALLEL:	Our dog Jolly is tiny, a rich brown coat, and a perky disposition.
PARALLEL:	Our dog Jolly is tiny, wears a rich brown coat, and has a perky disposition.
NOT PARALLEL:	A good driver obeys the speed limit, is alert, and she takes no risks on the road.
PARALLEL:	A good driver obeys the speed limit, is alert, and takes no risks on the road.

EXERCISE 18.   In each pair of sentences, point out the unified sentence or sentences. Tell why your choice is preferable.

1. *a.* I checked the bus schedule for the time of departure from Orlando and when the bus arrives at Tampa.

   b. I checked the bus schedule for the time of departure from Orlando and time of arrival at Tampa.

   _____

   _____

2. *a.* The path to the summit of Mt. Katahdin is rough, steep, and challenging.

   b. The path to the summit of Mt. Katahdin is rough, steep, and it is challenging.

   _____

   _____

3. *a.* Throughout the world, the number of languages is decreasing rapidly. Once there were more than a thousand languages in North and South America alone.

   b. Throughout the world, the number of languages is decreasing rapidly, and once there were more than a thousand languages in North and South America alone.

   _____

   _____

4. *a.* To run the domestic affairs of the White House, President Andrew Johnson depended on his daughter who bought two Jersey cows which provided fresh milk and butter which was used for the White House table.

   b. To run the domestic affairs of the White House, President Andrew Johnson depended on his daughter. She bought two Jersey cows to provide fresh milk and butter for the White House table.

   _____

   _____

5. *a.* The ideal dog is loyal, friendly, and is in good health.

   b. The ideal dog is loyal, friendly, and healthy.

   _____

   _____

EXERCISE 19.   Make each of the following unified. Follow the suggestions in the preceding pages.

1. The well-rounded tennis player has a good serve, a strong forehand, and he or she must have a dependable backhand.

   _____

   _____

2. The forty-first president of the United States, George H. Bush, is the father of the forty-third president, George W. Bush, and there was only one other father-son set who became presidents: John Adams and John Quincy Adams.

   _____

   _____

3. James Madison was the shortest President, who was only five feet four inches tall and who weighed only a hundred pounds.

   _____

   _____

4. A professional basketball player should be tall, agile, with a great deal of courage.

   _____

   _____

5. Four times the Wright brothers flew that first airbound plane which was finally struck by a gust of wind, which overturned it and wrecked it.

   _____

   _____

6. He gave the ticket that belonged to Lisa to Vadim, who kept it for a while but who then gave it to Jen, which was a surprise to her.

   _____

   _____

7. Ahmad practiced every day, and the contest demanded dedication from all those who entered it.

_____

_____

8. Sarah viewed the purpose of high school as learning, expanding her interests, and to have fun.

_____

_____

9. She slept in the bed which belonged to her grandmother, who left her many more things which were of great value and which other members of the family who were not as close to the grandmother wished they could have.

_____

_____

10. Carly enjoyed jogging, bicycling, and to hike.

_____

_____

Part THREE Common Usage Errors

We reviewed grammar and the parts of speech in Part One. We explored the structure of sentences in Part Two. Now we arrive at Part Three, which focuses on usage. What is "usage"? We may understand it as the customary, acceptable way in which words, phrases, and clauses are used in our language. More than simply a matter of language "manners," though, usage is a guide to clear, correct communication.

Lesson 20 Problems with Sentence Structure

There are three basic kinds of sentences: simple, compound, and complex. We already encountered these sentence types in Parts One and Two. Here, we learn about the parts of the sentences and how they work together. Along the way, you will have the opportunity to broaden your understanding with a little practice.

Simple Sentences

In Part One (pages 3–10) you learned that a sentence must have a **subject** and a **verb,** often called a **predicate.** In the following sentences, the subject has one line under it; the verb (predicate) has two.

> <u>Maria</u> <u>yelled</u>.

> A <u>section</u> of the bridge <u>fell</u> during the recent storm.

These are *simple sentences.* Each one contains a subject and a verb. Either the subject or the verb, or both, may be *compound.* Something that is compound has two or more parts. The following sentences have compound parts:

COMPOUND SUBJECT:	<u>Cindy</u> and <u>Jeffrey</u> smiled.
COMPOUND VERB:	Cindy <u>smiled</u> and <u>laughed</u>.
COMPOUND SUBJECT AND VERB:	<u>Cindy</u> and <u>Jeffrey</u> <u>smiled</u> and <u>laughed</u>.

EXERCISE 1.   Each numbered line consists of two sentences. Combine each pair into one simple sentence with compound parts. The finished sentence may have either a compound subject or a compound verb. (Be sure to make all necessary changes.)

1. Mario plays tennis. Carly also plays tennis.

   _____

   _____

2. The plane taxied on the runway. It finally stopped.

   _____

   _____

3. We visited Washington, D.C. We toured the city.

_____

_____

4. Jacy bought some new CDs. She stacked them on the shelf in her room.

_____

_____

5. The Tigers play their games in the city's stadium. The Lions, too, play their games in the city's stadium.

_____

_____

Compound Sentences

As we learned in Part One (pages 105–107), two or more *simple sentences* can be combined to form a *compound sentence*.

SIMPLE SENTENCE:	Dogs show affection for their owners.
SIMPLE SENTENCE:	Cats are more aloof.
COMPOUND SENTENCE:	Dogs show affection for their owners, but cats are more aloof.

The parts of a compound sentence are often joined together by **and, but, or,** or **nor.** These "joining words" are called *coordinating conjunctions.*

When two sentences are joined to make a compound sentence, the two main parts are called *clauses.* Because these two parts can stand by themselves as complete sentences, they are called *independent clauses.*

COMPOUND SENTENCE:	The bell rang, AND students quickly filled the halls.
COMPOUND SENTENCE:	Are you coming to the game, OR have you made other plans?
COMPOUND SENTENCE:	Rob doesn't like lima beans, NOR does he care for spinach. (To identify subject and verb, mentally arrange the sentence in subject-verb order: "he does care for spinach.")

EXERCISE 2.   Combine each pair of sentences to form a good compound sentence. Use **and, but, or,** or **nor.** Make slight changes in wording, if necessary.

1. You may think of Dobermans as vicious dogs. Many of them are gentle.

_____

_____

2. Tropical fish require great care. They may become sick and die.

_____

_____

3. Lightning struck the tree. The bark peeled off in layers.

_____

_____

4. Jim did not mow the lawn. He did not trim the hedges.

_____

_____

5. The rain poured down. The sun was shining.

_____

_____

Complex Sentences

We worked with *complex sentences* in Part Two (page 140) and saw how they can add interest and variety to writing. Now we look more closely at what makes a complex sentence. Like a compound sentence, a complex sentence has two or more clauses, but at least one of the clauses cannot stand by itself as a sentence. Note the following example:

COMPLEX SENTENCE:	If Paula calls, give her my message.
FIRST CLAUSE:	If Paula calls, (*subordinate clause*)
SECOND CLAUSE:	give her my message. (*independent clause*)

The *first clause* cannot function alone as a sentence. Although it has both a subject and a verb, it needs something to complete its thought. It is a **subordinate clause.** The *second clause* can stand by itself. It is an **independent clause** with the understood subject *you.*

Subordinate Clauses

Subordinate clauses can be difficult. Sometimes we make the mistake of punctuating them as if they were complete sentences. Then we end up with a *sentence fragment,* which will be covered in the next section (pages 155–164).

Subordinate clauses begin with connectives, or "joining words," called **subordinating conjunctions.** Here's a partial list:

after	before	than	until
although	how	though	when
as	if	till	while
because	since	unless	why

In the following sentences, the conjunctions are capitalized, the subordinate clauses are circled, and the independent clauses are underlined.

COMPLEX SENTENCE: <u>Juan went home</u> (WHEN the game ended.)

COMPLEX SENTENCE: (BEFORE the movie started,) <u>Kris bought popcorn.</u>

EXERCISE 3.

Circle the subordinate clause in each sentence. Draw a line under each clause that could stand by itself as a sentence.

1. After the TV show ended, I began my homework.

2. Natasha won't leave until Cindy arrives.

3. The rain will get heavier before it stops.

4. Although Jordan loves ice cream, he is going on a diet.

5. When the film is ready, pick it up from PhotoFlash.

More on Subordinate Clauses

Another type of subordinate clause begins with the pronoun **who, which,** or **that.** In the following sentences, the subordinate clauses are circled. You can see that they cannot stand by themselves as sentences.

COMPLEX SENTENCE: Ellen is the girl (WHO won the golf tournament.)

COMPLEX SENTENCE: The creamy filling, (WHICH is the best part of) (the cookie,) was eaten first.

COMPLEX SENTENCE: The part of the movie (THAT I liked best) was the ending.

EXERCISE 4.

Circle the subordinate clause in each sentence. Be careful not to circle part of the independent clause.

1. Caroline, who has not missed a school day in two years, is a friend of Sasha's.

2. The Statue of Liberty is the sight that has greeted millions of new immigrants.

3. Basketball, which was invented by an American, is now played around the world.

4. The violinist Itzhak Perlman is a man who has overcome serious physical disabilities.

5. One plant that everyone should avoid is poison ivy.

EXERCISE 5.   Identify each sentence by writing **Simple, Compound,** or **Complex** on the line.

1. The movie was good, but I enjoyed the book more.   _____

2. Her flight was canceled, and the trip was postponed.   _____

3. Katherine Lee, who was chosen to represent our
   school, could not attend the meeting.   _____

4. The teachers and the students stood together.   _____

5. The car skidded and almost struck a utility pole.   _____

6. Lisa replaced the glass that she had broken.   _____

7. Are you buying new clothes?   _____

8. He used his computer to make party invitations.   _____

9. When buses are delayed, students are usually late
   for school.   _____

10. Disneyland and Hollywood are popular places to
    visit in California.   _____

EXERCISE 6.   Combine each pair of sentences to make one complex sentence. If you need help, look again at the list of subordinating conjunctions on page 152.

1. The sunrise was beautiful. A storm rolled in by eleven.

   _____

   _____

2. Nick made it to class on time. Miranda was late.

   _____

   _____

3. Tom plays professional football. His brother is more talented in baseball.

   _____

   _____

4. My brothers Sean and Ian are going skiing. The snow is deep enough.

   _____

   _____

COMMON USAGE ERRORS

5. I left a note for the teacher. She never got my note.

_____

_____

6. I will have to wait a long time to buy my ticket. The line of people stretches for blocks.

_____

_____

7. Jeff is on the track team. He finished next to last in the first round of pole vault.

_____

_____

8. Don't forget to volunteer your time. The animal shelter needs a lot of help this time of year.

_____

_____

9. The lawyer rose slowly. The jury looked at him with expectation.

_____

_____

10. Carlo was studying in his room. Noisy construction was going on outside.

_____

_____

Sentence Fragments

One of the key skills you will need is the ability to write complete sentences. The sentence fragment is a pitfall to avoid.

Question: What is a sentence fragment?

Answer: When a group of words does not express a complete thought, it is a *sentence fragment.*

Here are some examples of them. Although they begin with a capital letter and have end punctuation, they are not complete sentences. Study ways they can be made into complete sentences.

NO VERB:	Raquel, along with a friend of hers from Dallas.
COMPLETE SENTENCE:	Raquel arrived, along with a friend of hers from Dallas.

NO VERB:	A small puppy running across the lawn. (The word *running* by itself is not a verb. It needs a helping verb like *is* or *was*. See Verbals as Fragments, page 161.)
COMPLETE SENTENCE:	A small puppy was running across the lawn.
NO SUBJECT:	Took the train from Boston to New Haven.
COMPLETE SENTENCE:	He took the train from Boston to New Haven.
NO VERB, NO SUBJECT:	From my uncle in Dallas.
COMPLETE SENTENCE:	I got a gift from my uncle in Dallas.

A common error is the use of a prepositional phrase as a complete sentence. A *preposition* relates the noun or pronoun following it to some other part of the sentence (see Lesson 14 in Part One, page 94). A *phrase* is a group of connected words that does not contain a subject or a predicate.

PREPOSITIONAL PHRASE:	Near the monitor on the desk.
COMPLETE SENTENCE:	An owner's manual lay near the monitor on the desk.

EXERCISE 7. Transform each sentence fragment into a complete sentence. Add words as needed.

1. At the bus stop on the corner near the Wal-Mart store.

   _____

   _____

2. Gabrielle, unhappy with the test results.

   _____

   _____

3. Lost my new watch somewhere in the locker room.

   _____

   _____

4. Enjoying the ski slopes of the Pocono Mountains.

   _____

   _____

5. The new Spike Lee film showing at a local theater.

   _____

   _____

6. An electric guitar in one corner and an amplifier in the other.

_____

_____

7. Carried the soccer equipment from the car to the garage.

_____

_____

8. The football team lining up for the kickoff.

_____

_____

9. Reaching first-period class as the bell rang.

_____

_____

10. The lead singer with the band behind him on the stage.

_____

_____

EXERCISE 8.   Change each sentence fragment into a complete sentence. Add whatever words are necessary.

1. Because I had never tasted tofu before.

_____

_____

2. A notebook lying on a bench in the locker room.

_____

_____

3. A deep freeze, a cause of many accidents on the slick roads.

_____

_____

4. Solved the third geometry problem after half an hour of hard work.

_____

_____

5. Along the bank of the Columbia River.

   _____

   _____

6. In the cafeteria, salads and sandwiches of all kinds.

   _____

   _____

7. Laughing at the funny parts in the movie.

   _____

   _____

8. Our best pitcher finding himself in trouble in the sixth inning.

   _____

   _____

9. Ran five laps around the track.

   _____

   _____

10. The autumn leaves in shades of yellow, red, and orange.

   _____

   _____

Subordinate Clauses as Fragments

Subordinate clauses, even though they have a subject and a verb, are not complete sentences (see page 152).

SUBORDINATE CLAUSE:	Unless you are here by six o'clock.
COMPLETE SENTENCE:	Unless you are here by six o'clock, I will have to leave.
SUBORDINATE CLAUSE:	When suddenly the traffic on Main Street came to a halt.
COMPLETE SENTENCE:	My family was driving home when suddenly the traffic on Main Street came to a halt.
SUBORDINATE CLAUSE:	Which have contributed to serious air pollution problems.
COMPLETE SENTENCE:	Many states have strict inspection and maintenance programs to control car exhaust emissions, which have contributed to serious air pollution problems.

A sentence fragment that consists of a subordinate clause can be corrected in two ways. One way is by eliminating the subordinating conjunction. The other way is by adding words to complete the thought.

SUBORDINATE CLAUSE:	When Julia won.
COMPLETE SENTENCE:	Julia won. (The subordinating conjunction *when* is eliminated.)
COMPLETE SENTENCE:	I was happy when Julia won. (Words are added to complete the thought.)

EXERCISE 9. Make each fragment into a complete sentence by eliminating the subordinating conjunction.

1. Although I had never seen Sakito before.

   _____

2. Unless Ethan changes his mind.

   _____

3. Why the refrigerator made a loud noise.

   _____

4. After we had packed our lunch for school.

   _____

5. Until the coach decides on a starting pitcher.

   _____

6. If a blizzard hits the city tonight.

   _____

7. Since you are a good friend of Allyson's.

   _____

8. When we won the first four games.

   _____

9. Since they got to school on time.

   _____

10. As the movie began.

    _____

EXERCISE 10. Make each fragment into a complete sentence by adding words to complete the thought.

1. When the clock struck twelve.

   _____

   _____

2. Because I live far away from school.

   _____

   _____

3. How I found my lost ring.

   _____

   _____

4. Since he had never taken American history before.

   _____

   _____

5. As the snow slowly drifted down from the sky.

   _____

   _____

6. Until Ted came with the key to the exercise room.

   _____

   _____

7. Whenever the dogs spotted a squirrel.

   _____

   _____

8. Before we arrived at the assembly.

   _____

   _____

9. Although Marissa doesn't usually like chocolate.

   _____

   _____

10. While Sergei was calling home.

   _____

   _____

Verbals as Fragments

Most of us play more than one role in life. You may be both a student and an athlete. Your father may be a gardener and a police officer. Your sister may be a singer and an actress. All three of you have different functions in each role. Playing two or more roles is a familiar part of life.

Some kinds of words also play two roles. A **verbal** is such a word. The suffix *al* means "like"; a verbal is *like a verb* but is not a verb. As the name suggests, it has a verb role, but it also acts as another part of speech. There are three different kinds of verbals: participles, gerunds, and infinitives (see Lesson 19, Part Two, pages 142–145). We now take a close look at each of these.

Participles

A participle acts as both a verb and an adjective.

> We found Darcy *painting* a mural.
> (*Painting* modifies *Darcy,* like an adjective, and takes an object, *mural,* like a verb.)

> *Exhausted* by the heat, we all jumped into the pool.
> (*Exhausted* modifies *we,* like an adjective, and in turn is modified by a prepositional phrase, *by the heat,* like a verb.)

> *Having pitched* a perfect game, Brian spoke to the reporters.
> (*Having pitched* modifies *Brian,* like an adjective, and takes an object, *game,* like a verb.)

A participle cannot make a complete sentence without a true verb.

NOT A SENTENCE:	Denyce jumping up and down with her diploma.
SENTENCE:	Denyce was jumping up and down with her diploma. (The helping verb *was* completes the verb.)
SENTENCE:	Denyce jumped up and down with her diploma.
NOT A SENTENCE:	Jaleel packing his gear for the rafting adventure.
SENTENCE:	Jaleel packed his gear for the rafting adventure.
SENTENCE:	Packing his gear for the rafting adventure, Jaleel threw in a change of clothes.

For how to avoid dangling modifiers, see Lesson 19, in Part Two, page 127.

Gerunds

A gerund acts as both a verb and a noun.

> I enjoy *riding* my bike early in the morning.
> (*Riding* is the object of *enjoy,* like a noun. It takes an object, *bike,* like a verb.)

> *Driving* a car in the city requires concentration and good nerves.
> (*Driving* is the subject of *requires,* like a noun. It takes an object, *car,* like a verb.)

A gerund cannot make a complete sentence without a true verb.

> NOT A SENTENCE: Winning the soccer match with a penalty kick.
>
> SENTENCE: Winning the soccer match with a penalty kick delighted the fans from Argentina.
>
> SENTENCE: Argentina won the soccer match with a penalty kick.

Infinitives

An infinitive can act as a noun, an adjective, or an adverb. An infinitive usually appears with *to*.

> Jeremy tried *to add* the solution to the glass beaker.
> (*To add* is the object of *tried*, like a noun. It takes an object, *solution*, like a verb.)
>
> The first student *to solve* the problem gets extra credit.
> (*To solve* modifies *student*, like an adjective. It has a direct object, *problem*, like a verb.)
>
> We used dry kindling *to start* the campfire.
> (*To start* modifies *used*, like an adverb. It takes an object, *campfire*, like a verb.)

An infinitive cannot make a complete sentence without a true verb.

> NOT A SENTENCE: To pick blackberries for a pie.
>
> SENTENCE: Cara decided to pick blackberries for a pie.
>
> SENTENCE: Cara picked blackberries for a pie.

EXERCISE 11. Each of the following uses a verbal in place of a verb. Write the verbal and tell what kind it is (participle, gerund, or infinitive).

Sample:

Ants crawling on the kitchen floor.

crawling; participle
_____

1. Our dog racing madly through the house in pursuit of our cat.

_____

2. To cut down a dead pine near the house.

_____

3. Finding a four-leaf clover in the back yard.

_____

4. Hoping for an answer to her letter.

_____

5. An electrician to rewire the old wing of the school.

_____

EXERCISE 12.   Each of the following uses a verbal in place of a verb. Rewrite each to make a complete sentence. Use the suggestions in the preceding pages.

1. To visit Rocky Mountain National Park this summer.

_____

_____

2. Dad frying hamburgers in a smoky kitchen.

_____

_____

3. Having wrapped the package neatly.

_____

_____

4. To warm up on a freezing winter's day.

_____

_____

5. Eating a healthy meal.

_____

_____

6. A good plan to get a great report card.

_____

_____

7. To see an opera for the first time.

_____

_____

8. Lying down in the wet grass.

_____

_____

9. Noticing a blind person on the corner of a busy intersection.

_____

_____

10. To apply for a part-time job in a fast-food restaurant.

_____

_____

Run-on Sentences

Writing sentence fragments is a serious error. Writing run-on sentences is an equally serious error.

Question: What is a run-on sentence?

Answer: A ***run-on sentence*** is two or more sentences written as if they were one sentence.

Sometimes sentences run on with no punctuation separating them, as in the first example following. Sometimes, as in the second example, a comma is present, but a comma is not strong enough to separate two complete sentences.

RUN-ON SENTENCE:	I enjoy computer games they keep me entertained on rainy days.
SEPARATE SENTENCES: (CORRECT)	I enjoy computer games. They keep me entertained on rainy days.
RUN-ON SENTENCE:	There was a loud splash, the dog had jumped into the pool.
SEPARATE SENTENCES: (CORRECT)	There was a loud splash. The dog had jumped into the pool.

EXERCISE 13. Rewrite the following run-on sentences. Make them into two separate sentences.

1. That piano is beautiful, it has a beautiful sound, too.

_____

_____

2. Maria enjoys swimming her brother Raoul prefers sailing and fishing.

_____

_____

3. Can we leave now do you have the tickets?

_____

_____

4. I don't like most television comedies, they are boring.

_____

_____

5. The business of renting DVDs is popular there are two new rental stores in town.

_____

_____

6. Galina forgot her lunch she will have to buy one.

_____

_____

7. Jason found his lost calculator, it was in an old backpack.

_____

_____

8. I would love to see that show, the tickets are so expensive, though.

_____

_____

9. It began to rain hard, the hail started a few minutes later.

_____

_____

10. In some places, there is no summer vacation can you imagine it?

_____

_____

11. The teacher knew he was smart, he just did not work hard.

_____

_____

12. Caitlyn knew that Jared wanted to go to the game he loved football so much.

_____

_____

13. My dog thinks he's human, he would sit at the kitchen table with us if we let him!

_____

_____

14. Do you think Janine would like the necklace it's so pretty.

_____

_____

15. It's nice outside, let's go for a run.

_____

_____

Change Run-on Sentences to Compound and Complex Sentences

Some run-on sentences can be corrected by adding an appropriate connecting word.

RUN-ON SENTENCE:	Video games require good coordination, players must react quickly.
COMPOUND SENTENCE: (CORRECT)	Video games require good coordination, and players must react quickly.
RUN-ON SENTENCE:	Britney goes to summer school, she has to improve her math grade.
COMPLEX SENTENCE: (CORRECT)	Britney goes to summer school because she has to improve her math grade.

The following words can lead to run-on sentences: *also, hence, nevertheless, nonetheless, furthermore, then, therefore,* and *thus.* These words are not conjunctions (they are adverbs). They cannot join sentences with only a comma. Sometimes a semicolon is used.

RUN-ON SENTENCE:	The driver stopped, then he got out of his car.
SEPARATE SENTENCES: (CORRECT)	The driver stopped. Then he got out of his car.
RUN-ON SENTENCE:	My best subject is science, therefore I took a science elective this year.
WITH SEMICOLON: (CORRECT)	My best subject is science; therefore, I took a science elective this year.

COMMON USAGE ERRORS

EXERCISE 14. Change the following run-on sentences into compound or complex ones.

1. The Buccaneers are a winning team, they have a good defense.

   _____

   _____

2. Maryanne practiced her ballet routine for two hours, she is in a special performance.

   _____

   _____

3. The light was shining in my eyes, I pulled the shade down.

   _____

   _____

4. Jean-Claude ran into the supermarket, he went to the bakery section.

   _____

   _____

5. Julie was driving too fast, she slowed down when her mother told her to.

   _____

   _____

6. I opened the door the phone rang.

   _____

   _____

7. Rosita got a good grade on the French test, she studied very hard.

   _____

   _____

8. Mr. Carson doesn't jog every day, he doesn't golf anymore.

   _____

   _____

9. Shake the bottle of cold medicine, take two tablespoons, as the directions say.

   _____

   _____

10. She listened to the CD player, she had earphones on.

   _____

   _____

We have focused on sentences in this lesson—types of sentences and how to form them, as well as those troubling sentence fragments and run-on sentences. The following two exercises offer some more practice on what we have learned.

EXERCISE 15. Eliminate all sentence fragments. Correct the run-on sentences. Add or eliminate words as needed.

1. If she were elected president of the Spanish Club.

   _____

   _____

2. Have you ever seen the locks on the St. Lawrence Seaway, they are fascinating.

   _____

   _____

3. With a cry of victory at the end of the long, hard tennis match.

   _____

   _____

4. Visited my grandmother in Greenville.

   _____

   _____

5. The dog barked noisily, then a car pulled into the driveway.

   _____

   _____

6. Why don't you plan a visit to the American Museum of Natural History, it has a fantastic collection of gems.

   _____

   _____

7. When a duck and her five ducklings waddled across the street.

   _____

   _____

8. Four runners standing in the starting line.

   _____

   _____

9. Which had been closed for repairs.

_____

_____

10. The boy's team won four of their matches the girls' team won five of theirs.

_____

_____

11. Having gotten a good night's sleep.

_____

_____

12. The car was packed we left on vacation.

_____

_____

13. The movie that was chosen as best picture of the year.

_____

_____

14. Close the door let's go.

_____

_____

15. The senior class trip is to Disney World, is your brother going?

_____

_____

EXERCISE 16.   Follow the directions carefully to create the sentences requested.

Sample:

Write a complex sentence with a subordinate clause beginning with *unless*.

Unless Daria cleaned her room, she wasn't allowed to have a television in it.

1. Write a simple sentence with a compound subject.

_____

_____

2. Write a compound sentence.

_____

_____

3. Write a complex sentence.

_____

_____

4. Write a complex sentence with a subordinate clause beginning with *that*.

_____

_____

5. Write a simple sentence with a compound subject and a compound verb.

_____

_____

6. Write a compound sentence using *or*.

_____

_____

7. Write a simple sentence with a compound verb.

_____

_____

8. Write a complex sentence with two subordinate clauses.

_____

_____

9. Write a sentence with a subordinate clause beginning with *if*.

_____

_____

10. Write a complex sentence with two independent clauses.

_____

_____

Lesson 21 Problems with Nouns

Recall from Lesson 4 in Part One (pages 27–37) that there are two main problems with nouns. The first is forming *plurals*. The second is forming *possessives*. When you have to form plural possessives, you are faced with both problems. This lesson provides some extra practice for both.

Plurals of Nouns

Rules for forming plural nouns were given in Lessons 4 (pages 28–34) and 10 (page 63) in Part One. You may wish to review these before trying your hand at Exercises 1 through 3.

EXERCISE 1.   Write the plural form of each of the following nouns.

1. baby _____

2. bunch _____

3. crash _____

4. puff _____

5. glass _____

6. half _____

7. miss _____

8. pinch _____

9. pony _____

10. stone _____

11. story _____

12. tank _____

13. tray _____

14. key _____

15. wax _____

EXERCISE 2.   Form the plural of each of the following nouns.

1. mouthful _____

2. echo _____

3. foot _____

4. textbook _____

5. sheep _____

6. piano _____

7. roof _____   9. potato _____

8. hero _____   10. tooth _____

EXERCISE 3. Write the plurals for these nouns.

1. strawberry _____   6. saleswoman _____

2. chef _____   7. branch _____

3. government _____   8. attorney _____

4. bookshelf _____   9. family _____

5. radio _____   10 foot _____

Possessives of Nouns

The formation of possessive nouns was explained in Lesson 4 (pages 34–37) in Part One. It may be a good idea to turn back to that lesson and review how to form singular and plural possessives. Some practice exercises follow.

EXERCISE 4. Write the singular possessive form of each of the following nouns.

1. animal _____   7. igloo _____

2. attorney-general _____   8. sister _____

3. brother _____   9. nurse _____

4. commander in chief _____   10. week _____

5. fox _____   11. man _____

6. girl _____   12. year _____

EXERCISE 5. Write the plural possessive form of each of the following nouns. *Remember:* First write the plural. Then add an ' or s' as needed.

1. athlete _____   5. goose _____

2. city _____   6. house _____

3. salesman _____   7. mouse _____

4. four-year-old _____   8. month _____

9. parent _____   11. tree _____

10. search _____   12. wolf _____

   Now, practice forming both plurals and possessives in the next two exercises.

EXERCISE 6. Write the singular possessive, plural, and plural possessive of each of the following nouns.

SINGULAR	SINGULAR POSSESSIVE	PLURAL	PLURAL POSSESSIVE
1. book	_____	_____	_____
2. man	_____	_____	_____
3. box	_____	_____	_____
4. punch	_____	_____	_____
5. calf	_____	_____	_____
6. cage	_____	_____	_____
7. pie	_____	_____	_____
8. ox	_____	_____	_____
9. mouse	_____	_____	_____
10. deer	_____	_____	_____
11. soprano	_____	_____	_____
12. athlete	_____	_____	_____
13. story	_____	_____	_____
14. monkey	_____	_____	_____
15. thief	_____	_____	_____

EXERCISE 7. Write the correct form of the noun in parentheses as required by the sense of the sentence.

1. He left two of his (*book*) _____ on the bus.

2. The (*book*) _____ cover was torn.

3. Bill drove his (*sister*) _____ car.

4. The two (*sister*) _____ started two (*business*)
   _____.

5. I saw three (*goose*) _____ swimming in the pond.

6. The park ranger noticed that many of the (*goose*) _____ wings
   were missing feathers.

7. Two of Mr. Dixon's (*daughter*) _____ own a computer store.

8. The two (*daughter*) _____ store is on Main Street.

9. Both of my (*brother*) _____ belong to the (*school*) _____
   basketball team.

10. Ten of the hotel's (*doorman*) _____ worked on Sunday.

Lesson 22 Problems with Verbs

Every sentence has at least one verb. When you construct sentences, you have to pay close attention to the verbs. You must choose the correct tense of the verb and make the verb agree with its subject. The following discussion centers on these aspects of verbs. The lesson ends with a review of some verb pairs that are especially troublesome.

Using the Correct Tense

Question: What is "tense"?

Answer: *Tense* means "time."

The form of a verb shows the time of the action that the verb expresses. Be sure to use the correct tense in your writing.

PRESENT TENSE:	A statue of Thomas Jefferson *stands* in Washington, D.C.
PAST TENSE:	The Tampa Bay Buccaneers *won* the Super Bowl in 2003.
FUTURE TENSE:	Taryn *will go* to the dentist at five o'clock this afternoon.
PRESENT PERFECT TENSE:	The Pyramids *have lasted* for thousands of years.
PAST PERFECT TENSE:	By late afternoon, all the guests *had left*.
FUTURE PERFECT TENSE:	By the year 2020, people's taste in popular music *will have changed*.

Staying with the Same Tense

A common mistake is to mix the present and the past in a sentence. Stick to the same tense. Study the two examples to see how to correct errors.

MIXED TENSES:	I <u>lose</u> my keys and <u>waited</u> for my mother to come home.
	present *past*
SAME TENSE:	I <u>lose</u> my keys and <u>wait</u> for my mother to come home.
	present *present*
SAME TENSE:	I <u>lost</u> my keys and <u>waited</u> for my mother to come home.
	past *past*

MIXED TENSES: Because she <u>misses</u> the bus, she <u>walked</u> to school.
                          present   *past*

SAME TENSE: Because she <u>misses</u> the bus, she <u>walks</u> to school.
                          present   *present*

SAME TENSE: Because she <u>missed</u> the bus, she <u>walked</u> to school.
                          past   *past*

EXERCISE 1.   The following sentences show inconsistent use of tense, mixing present and past. Make each pair of verbs consistent.

In 1–3, make all verbs present tense.

1. I get up at 7:00 A.M. and took a quick shower.

   _____

   _____

2. Children splashed in the neighborhood pool while the lifeguards watch carefully.

   _____

   _____

3. She turned off the soap opera as her brother comes through the door.

   _____

   _____

In 4–6, make all verbs past tense.

4. The school bus was late, but I get an excuse note from the driver.

   _____

   _____

5. We hike up the Mt. Greylock trail and rested on the summit.

   _____

   _____

6. I asked our football coach to put me in the game, but he says my arm isn't rested enough.

   _____

   _____

In 7–9, make all verbs present tense.

7. Cai strolls into the cafeteria and sat down next to Page.

   _____

   _____

8. Alex walked confidently to the front of the room and speaks to the class.

    _____

    _____

9. My sister handed the clarinet to me and then cringes when I try to play it.

    _____

    _____

In 10–12, make all verbs past tense.

10. Ben thinks for a moment and then explained his point of view.

    _____

    _____

11. The 727 departed from O'Hare International Airport and then heads toward Atlanta.

    _____

    _____

12. The players slip up behind the winning coach and dumped a bucket of Gatorade on him.

    _____

    _____

Principal Parts of Verbs

Question: What do we mean by "principal parts"?

Answer: The *principal parts* of a verb are those parts used to form tenses.

Except for helping verbs (*can, be, may, have,* etc.), all English verbs have four principal parts—the infinitive (without the "to"), present, past, and past participle. In our language, verbs can be regular or irregular.

Regular Verbs

Most verbs are *regular*. They form tenses (express time of an action) in regular, predictable ways.

> I **play** my music loudly.
>> (Expresses an action taking place or an action always true; *play* is present tense.)

> I **played** my music loudly.
>> (Expresses an action gone by; *played* is past tense.)

> I have **played** my music loudly.
>> (Expresses an action completed at the time of speaking; *have played* is a helping verb, *have,* plus the past participle *played.*)

Irregular Verbs

Some verbs are *irregular*. They cause trouble because they do not form their tenses in the usual way.

> **I see** a UFO.
>> (Expresses an action taking place; *see* is present tense.)

> **I saw** a UFO.
>> (Expresses an action gone by; *saw* is past tense.)

> I have **seen** a UFO.
>> (Expresses an action completed at the time of speaking; *have seen* is a helping verb, *have*, plus the past participle *seen*.)

Principal Parts of Irregular Verbs

A speaker or writer of correct English must know the principal parts of irregular verbs. For example,

> WE DON'T SAY: We swimmed to the shore.
> WE DO SAY: We **swam** to the shore.

> WE DON'T SAY: Mom has went to the office.
> WE DO SAY: Mom **has gone** to the office. (*Has* is a helping verb.)

> WE DON'T SAY: The girls have ate their lunch.
> WE DO SAY: The girls **have eaten** their lunch. (*Have* is a helping verb.)

Here is a list of the trickiest irregular verbs. Study them thoroughly.

PRINCIPAL PARTS OF 40 IRREGULAR VERBS

PRESENT	PAST	PAST PARTICIPLE
am	was	(have) been
become	became	(have) become
begin	began	(have) begun
blow	blew	(have) blown
break	broke	(have) broken
bring	brought	(have) brought
catch	caught	(have) caught
choose	chose	(have) chosen
come	came	(have) come
do	did	(have) done
draw	drew	(have) drawn
drink	drank	(have) drunk

drive	drove	(have) driven
eat	ate	(have) eaten
fall	fell	(have) fallen
find	found	(have) found
freeze	froze	(have) frozen
get	got	(have) gotten *or* got
give	gave	(have) given
go	went	(have) gone
hold	held	(have) held
know	knew	(have) known
lay	laid	(have) laid
leave	left	(have) left
lie	lay	(have) lain
ride	rode	(have) ridden
rise	rose	(have) risen
say	said	(have) said
see	saw	(have) seen
shake	shook	(have) shaken
sit	sat	(have) sat
speak	spoke	(have) spoken
stick	stuck	(have) stuck
swim	swam	(have) swum
take	took	(have) taken
teach	taught	(have) taught
tear	tore	(have) torn
throw	threw	(have) thrown
win	won	(have) won
wind	wound	(have) wound
write	wrote	(have) written

Forms of *have* and of *be* and *do* are often used as helping verbs: *has left, were chosen, do agree*.

EXERCISE 2. In each sentence, underline the correct form of the verb.

1. Evan (**brought, brung**) his Jack Russell terrier to the picnic.

2. Manuela has (**chose, chosen**) dramatics as her English elective.

3. Mr. Esposito (**did, done**) a good job in landscaping his yard.

4. You missed Tanya. She has (**gone, went**) to the movies.

5. Oh no, I've (**tore, torn**) my jacket.

6. I (**been, have been**) taking tennis lessons this summer.

7. The old maple tree in our yard has (**fallen, fell**) at last.

8. Todd (**came, come**) late to the rehearsal yesterday.

9. That unopened book has (**laid, lain**) on the desk for a week.

10. Yesterday's storm has (**shaken, shook**) most of the apples from the tree.

11. Chan (**swam, swum**) forty laps in the pool yesterday.

12. Have you (**gave, given**) clothes you've outgrown to the Salvation Army?

13. As we left for the beach, the sky (**began, begun**) to darken.

14. During our move to Phoenix, three of our lamps were (**broke, broken**).

15. Paolo thought he (**knew, knowed**) the girl who had just entered the store.

16. Has any quarterback ever (**throwed, thrown**) a football 80 yards?

17. The weather at the soccer game turned cold, and we were nearly (**froze, frozen**).

18. "Saving Our Rainforests" is the best composition Doreen has ever (**written, wrote**).

19. Have you ever (**spoke, spoken**) before a full auditorium?

20. The quarterback (**saw, seen**) a free receiver and completed the pass.

21. Linda had (**drew, drawn**) a picture of the old schoolhouse.

22. I was so thirsty I (**drank, drunk**) a whole quart of lemonade.

23. Get up! The sun has already (**risen, rose**).

24. Until yesterday, Dad had never (**driven, drove**) a sports car.

25. Christina (**did, done**) a good job with that craft work.

26. Kamali has (**chose, chosen**) her courses for next year.

27. Have you ever (**ridden, rode**) in an old car over bumpy roads?

28. The wind has (**blowed, blown**) hard all night long.

29. Colleen (**began, begun**) to have doubts about arriving on time in Memphis.

30. I had never (**ate, eaten**) chickpeas before yesterday.

Agreement of Subject and Verb

Question: What is *agreement?*

Answer: A verb must agree with its subject in *number*. That is, if the subject of a sentence is singular, the verb must also be singular: "The *child is* lost." If the subject is plural, the verb must also be plural: "Your *friends are* here."

	SINGULAR	PLURAL
First Person:	I enjoy	we enjoy
Second Person:	you enjoy	you enjoy
Third Person:	he, she, it enjoys	they enjoy

The verb *to be*, the commonest verb in English, is, unfortunately, irregular. These are the present tense forms:

First Person:	I am	we are
Second Person:	you are	you are
Third Person:	he, she, it is	they are

These are the past tense forms:

I was	we were
you were	you were
he, she, it was	they were

The important verb *to have* is worth a look. These are the present tense forms:

First Person:	I have	we have
Second Person:	you have	you have
Third Person:	he, she, it has	they have

These are the past tense forms:

I had	we had
you had	you had
he, she, it had	they had

Most native speakers of English tend to use the right form in sentences in which the verb follows the subject. Here is an example:

A <u>tree</u> <u>stands</u> at the front gate.

In other sentences, subject-verb agreement is not as simple as in the sentence above, and mistakes are commonly made. Study the following few rules; they will help you avoid such mistakes.

1. **Confusion can result when there are words** (those in parentheses below) **between the subject and the verb.**

   A <u>tree</u> (with green leaves) <u>stands</u> at the front gate.

   Some people would mistakenly write *stand* in the belief that *leaves* is the subject. It is not.

2. **Expressions like *with, together with, according to, including, as well as, plus,* and *no less than* do not affect subject-verb agreement.**

   The <u>coach</u>, as well as the players, <u>is going</u> to the game by plane.

   Coach is the subject, not *players* (or *coach and players*).

3. **Another common difficulty arises when the subject is compound. The words *and, or, nor, either . . . or, neither . . . nor* signal the presence of a compound subject.**

   a. **When two subjects are connected by *and*, the subject is plural and the verb is usually plural.**

      High <u>seas</u> AND dense <u>fog</u> <u>have slowed</u> the rescue operation.

   b. **When two singular subjects are joined by *or* or *nor*, the subject is singular and the verb is singular.**

      An <u>apple</u> OR an <u>orange</u> <u>was</u> in every box lunch.

   c. **When two subjects of different number are joined by *neither . . . nor* or *either . . . or*, the verb agrees with the nearer subject.**

NEITHER <u>Stacy</u> NOR her <u>brothers</u> <u>are going</u> to the state convention.

EITHER these telephone <u>numbers</u> OR that <u>address</u> <u>is</u> wrong.

4. *You* **always takes a plural verb. "You was" is wrong.**

<u>You</u> <u>were listed</u> on today's honor roll.

<u>Were</u> <u>you</u> <u>expecting</u> the honor?

5. **When the subject comes after the verb, find the subject and make the verb agree with it.**

(**Was, Were**) the nominees for Best Actor all present at the Academy Awards ceremony?
(The subject is *nominees*. Therefore, *were* is correct.)

There (**was, were**) three raccoons digging in the trash heap.
(The subject is *raccoons*, not the introductory word *there*. *Were* is correct. *Here* is a similar introductory word.)

In a corner of my desk (**are, is**) the schedules for the Spurs' basketball games and the Bears' football games.
(The subject is *schedules*. *Are* is correct.)

EXERCISE 3. In each sentence, underline the correct form of the verb.

1. The books on that shelf (**are, is**) biographies.

2. The coach, together with his players, (**are, is**) having pictures taken.

3. The elm and the chestnut (**is, are**) subject to a deadly disease.

4. Neither the president nor the other officers (**was, were**) present at the lecture.

5. A good food for dogs (**contain, contains**) the right balance of vitamins and minerals.

6. Either the Denby brothers or Wu Chen (**are, is**) my choice for first place in the competition.

7. The door as well as the windows (**was, were**) locked.

8. A woman representing local consumer organizations (**speak, speaks**) tonight in the auditorium.

9. The two computers in my father's study (**are, is**) old but still in working order.

10. A yogurt or an apple (**are, is**) not enough for lunch.

11. I was happy when you (**was, were**) chosen class president.

12. There (**was, were**) several garnets in that rock you found.

13. On top of the mountain (**are, is**) two huge boulders, easily seen from below.

14. Here (**come, comes**) the winners!

15. (**Was, Were**) you surprised to find your watch in that old jacket?

EXERCISE 4.   In each sentence, underline the correct form of the verb.

1. Jennie Lynn (**doesn't, don't**) know whether or not to get her hair cut short.

2. The front tires of your sister's car (**are, is**) worn and smooth.

3. The first clock to strike the hours (**was, were**) constructed in 1754 by Benjamin Banneker.

4. Aunt Ginny, with her two daughters, (**are, is**) arriving on the ten o'clock train from Danville.

5. Fog, with poor visibility, (**are, is**) often a problem on the coast.

6. There (**was, were**) several good scoring opportunities in the playoff game between the Pirates and the Reds.

7. At the Halloween party, (**was, were**) you the vampire with the long cloak?

8. At the intersection of Church Street and Main (**are, is**) two new stores.

9. Four questions on the biology test (**are, is**) really difficult.

10. Heavy rainfall during September and October (**help, helps**) to keep down forest fires.

11. One of the twins (**are, is**) taking Russian next year.

12. Neither the coach nor his assistants (**was, were**) available for an interview after the game.

13. Either broccoli or asparagus (**are, is**) perfect for tonight's dinner.

14. In the barn (**was, were**) two ancient tractors still in good running order.

15. (**Was, Were**) there any doughnuts left after the meeting?

Troublesome Verb Pairs

Some verb pairs cause more than their share of problems. Learn the correct use of each verb in the following pairs.

Lie, Lay

First, study the forms of these tricky verbs.

PRESENT	PRESENT PARTICIPLE	PAST	PAST PARTICIPLE
lie ("rest," "recline")	lying	lay	lain
lay ("put" or "set down")	laying	laid	laid

Now notice these correct forms:

Angela is *lying* down. She *lay* down an hour ago. She has *lain* on the couch without moving.

Mr. Winters is *laying* the tile. He *laid* most of the tile yesterday. He has *laid* tile for a number of builders.

Sit, Set

PRESENT	PRESENT PARTICIPLE	PAST	PAST PARTICIPLE
sit ("occupy a chair")	sitting	sat	sat
set ("place," "put in order")	setting	set	set

Here are examples of the correct forms:

My grandmother is *sitting* on the front porch. She *sat* in her favorite rocker. She has *sat* in that chair many times.

The twins are *setting* the table. They *set* it this morning, too. They have *set* it for every meal this week.

Bring, Take

To bring usually calls for motion toward the speaker. *To take* usually calls for motion away from the speaker. The following sentences use these verbs correctly:

When you come home from school today, please *bring* me the evening paper.

Please *take* this overdue book to the library.

Imply, Infer

You may hear these words used interchangeably. They should not be. To *imply* is to suggest. To *infer* is to draw a conclusion or to guess. The examples below show correct usage:

His presence *implied* agreement with the decision.

I *inferred* from his presence that he agreed.

Affect, Effect

This pair of easily confused words could very well get top honors as the most troublesome. Not only are both words verbs—they also are nouns.

Affect as a verb means to influence, have an effect on. *Effect* as a verb means to accomplish or bring about. *Effect* is sometimes mistakenly used when *affect* should be. Look at the examples carefully.

Too much television watching *affected* Skye's grades.

Increased study time in the evening *effected* an improvement in Skye's grades.

Most of the time you will use *affect* as the verb.

Even though this lesson focuses on verbs, we will touch on the noun confusion here as well. You may often see *affect* used when *effect* is meant. An *effect* is a consequence or result of something. *Affect* is a more specialized term from psychology that refers to feelings or emotions as opposed to thoughts and actions. If it does crop up in ordinary conversation or writing, most often it is used in connection with an absence of emotion. Consider the following:

The movie had a good *effect* on Lee's bad mood.

Her *affect* was so blunted, we could not make her laugh.

Do not worry too much about *affect* as a noun. Only rarely, if ever, will you use it. Do, however, learn the distinction between the verbs *affect* and *effect*. Not doing so will surely affect (NOT effect) your grade.

EXERCISE 5.   In each sentence, underline the correct form in parentheses.

1. Wake up Dad. He has (**laid, lain**) in that hammock all afternoon.

2. At my brother's graduation, our family was (**setting, sitting**) in the third row of the auditorium.

3. She (**implied, inferred**) from Mr. Giovanni's smile that she had answered correctly.

4. Please (**bring, take**) this saw down to the workbench in the basement.

5. A bird (**sits, sets**) on its eggs to hatch them.

6. The book was right where he (**lay, laid**) it last week.

7. What are you (**implying, inferring**) by saying that?

8. I would like to (**lie, lay**) down now.

9. Losing the quarterback to injury will have a bad (**effect, affect**) on the team.

10. Tam hoped that her one bad test grade would not (**effect, affect**) the teacher's opinion of her.

EXERCISE 6.   On line (*b*), rewrite sentence (*a*) by changing the agreement of the subject and verb. If the subject is singular, make it plural. If it is plural, make it singular. The first one is done for you.

1. *a.* Emily walks to the library.

   b. Emily and Bill walk to the library.

2. *a.* Two rosebushes grow by the door.

   b. _____

3. *a.* Chase plays baseball.

   b. _____

4. *a.* The whistle blows at noon.

   b. _____

5. *a.* The bill is overdue.

   b. _____

EXERCISE 7.   In each sentence, underline the correct form of the verb.

1. Our cat Tigger has been (**laying, lying**) in that chair all afternoon.

2. With a smile, my mother (**implied, inferred**) that I was getting a birthday surprise.

3. All four paws and the tail of the black kitten (**was, were**) black.

4. Our lazy puppy Tagalong (**laid, lay**) in the sun.

5. Please (**bring, take**) this hostess gift to Mrs. Hancock.

6. It (**doesn't, don't**) matter if you can't finish the book by Friday.

7. The barn, with the surrounding buildings, (**was, were**) threatened by the brush fire.

8. Granddad is (**setting, sitting**) on the front porch, watching the world go by.

9. When (**was, were**) you finally able to finish your term paper?

10. Either the encyclopedia or the unabridged dictionary (**are, is**) likely to have a map of post–Iron Curtain Europe.

11. There (**are, is**) many great recipes for spaghetti with marinara sauce.

12. It was a lazy day, and we (**laid, lay**) on the beach most of the morning.

13. Don't think that sleeping through class won't (**effect, affect**) your report card.

14. She (**sat, set**) her paper on the counter—and then forgot it.

15. An Abyssinian cat and a Himalayan cat (**are, is**) pictured on a single United States stamp.

COMMON USAGE ERRORS

Lesson 23 Problems with Modifiers

Nouns and verbs carry the essential thought of a sentence. These are the bread-and-butter words, the key content words, the power words. Other kinds of words, called *modifiers,* add exactness and color to sentences. Notice the difference they make.

1. Monkeys chattered.

2. A hundred monkeys chattered noisily.

The bare sentence in 1 is made much more vivid by the added modifiers in sentence 2. We call these modifiers adjectives and adverbs.

Question: What do adjectives and adverbs do?

Answer: An *adjective* modifies (tells something about) a noun. An *adverb* modifies (tells something about) a verb. In sentence 2, *hundred*, an adjective, modifies the noun *monkeys*. *Noisily*, an adverb, modifies the verb *chattered*.

Recall that Part One extensively discussed adjectives (Lessons 11 and 13) and adverbs (Lessons 12 and 13)—how they function, how they differ, and how some adverbs are formed from adjectives. In this lesson, we touch on a couple of usage concerns.

Adjectives and Adverbs Confused

Part One pointed out that a common problem with modifiers is to confuse adjectives with adverbs. The usual error is to use an adjective when an adverb is needed. Look at the following sentences.

1. Pierce did *well* on his science test. (NOT *good*)

2. Taborri sometimes speaks too *rapidly*. (NOT *rapid*)

3. Young birds in nests must be fed *regularly*. (NOT *regular*)

4. Meghan looked *thoughtfully* at her test paper before beginning to write. (NOT *thoughtful*)

5. To teach tricks to any animal, you must work *patiently* with it. (NOT *patient*)

In each sentence, underline the correct modifier in parentheses.

1. You cannot do (**good, well**) if you don't have enough sleep.

2. The runaway truck lurched (**wild, wildly**) down the road before running into a ditch.

3. After only two lessons, Marie-Louise plays golf very (**good, well**).

4. The river current was rushing too (**swift, swiftly**) for safe swimming.

5. Our relay team ran (**good, well**), but we still came in second.

6. Please travel (**safe, safely**) at night.

7. After his accident, he walks as (**good, well**) as can be expected.

8. Naina finished the Spanish test (**quick, quickly**).

9. She spoke (**loud, loudly**).

10. Mike did (**bad, badly**) on his driver's test.

Double Negatives

A **negative** is a "no" word such as *no, not, never, nobody, nothing, hardly,* or *scarcely.* The *n't* in a contraction (as in *don't*) is a negative. A **double negative** occurs when TWO negatives are mistakenly used to make one negative statement. The remedy? Simply remove one of the negatives.

The examples below show two ways of removing one of the negative words.

NEGATIVES

Two: I do<u>n't</u> have <u>no</u> homework tonight.

One: I have <u>no</u> homework tonight.

One: I do<u>n't</u> have any homework tonight.

Two: Juan is<u>n't</u> going to have <u>nothing</u> to do with you.

One: Juan is going to have <u>nothing</u> to do with you.

One: Juan is<u>n't</u> going to have anything to do with you.

Two: Do<u>n't</u> <u>never</u> read the final pages of a thriller first.

One: <u>Never</u> read the final pages of a thriller first.

One: Do<u>n't</u> ever read the final pages of a thriller first.

Two: There are<u>n't</u> <u>hardly</u> any sandwiches left.

One: There are <u>hardly</u> any sandwiches left.

One: There are almost <u>no</u> sandwiches left.

Two:	Nobody isn't left to play goalie.
One:	Nobody is left to play goalie.
One:	There isn't anybody left to play goalie.

Either change a negative word to its opposite (for example, *nothing* to *anything*, *never* to *ever*, *no* to *any*) or eliminate a negative contraction. Do not do both, though. You will end up with a sentence that makes no sense, such as "I have any homework tonight."

EXERCISE 2. In each sentence, underline the correct word in parentheses.

1. That haircut makes Brian look as if he hasn't (**any, no**) hair.

2. There isn't (**any, no**) more iced tea in the jug.

3. Paulina doesn't go (**anywhere, nowhere**) without her pocket calculator.

4. The light was so dim I (**could, couldn't**) hardly read the message.

5. Don't (**ever, never**) cross the street against the light.

EXERCISE 3. In each sentence, underline the correct modifier in parentheses.

1. Don't answer too (**rapid, rapidly**).

2. The gymnast performed her routine (**careful, carefully**).

3. The car (**isn't, is**) hardly moving.

4. Jay doesn't have (**any, no**) work to do tonight.

5. That second contestant sang really (**good, well**).

6. You don't get (**anywhere, nowhere**) with a bad attitude.

7. Juma isn't saying (**nothing, anything**) about why he was absent.

8. He knew how to solve the chemistry problem (**simple, simply**).

9. I felt relieved when the robot worked (**good, well**) at the science fair.

10. Cameron was considerate and played the music (**soft, softly**).

Other Errors

1. Don't add *s* **to** *anyway, anywhere, everywhere, nowhere, somewhere.*

My Spanish book must be somewhere̸ around here.

2. **Don't say *this here* or *that there* to describe a noun.**

    This ~~here~~ cake was made without eggs.

3. **Don't use *more* with an *-er* word (*more wiser*) or *most* with an *-est* word (*most prettiest*).**

    Our cat is ~~more~~ smarter than our cocker spaniel.

Lesson 24 Problems with Pronouns

Personal Pronouns

Subjects and Objects

A handful of pronouns cause more trouble than all the rest put together. These *personal pronouns,* as you may recall from Part One, Lesson 9, have different forms when they are used as subjects and as objects. There is plenty of room for confusion. Because these pronouns can be so tricky, this lesson reviews some basic guidelines for getting them right.

Here are the troublemakers:

	Singular			*Plural*	
As subjects:	I	he	she	we	they
As objects:	me	him	her	us	them

Notice that these pronouns are paired. Your choice in a sentence would be between *I* and *me,* for example. *I* is the form used for the subject and *me* for the object.

> *I* watched the Bears game Monday night.
> (*I* is the subject of the verb *watched.*)

> Steve told *me* about the surprise party for Luis.
> (*Me* is the object of the verb *told.*)

Most pronoun difficulties occur when two pronouns are joined by *and.* When in doubt, say what you would say if each pronoun stood alone.

> Laura and *she* (not *her*) competed in the debate.

> Say:
> Laura competed.
> She competed.
> Laura and she (not *her*) competed. *Laura* and *she* form a compound SUBJECT.

> Mr. Foster gave Mollie and *me* (not *I*) a chance to play in the mixed-doubles tournament. (*Note:* It is courteous to mention the other person first: "Mollie and me," NOT "me and Mollie.")

Say:

    Mr. Foster gave Mollie.
    Mr. Foster gave me.
    Mr. Foster gave Mollie and me (not *I*). *Mollie* and *me* form a
    compound indirect OBJECT.

Go with Maura and *him* (not *he*) to the flea market.

    Say:

    Go with Maura.
    Go with him.
    Go with Maura and him (not *he*). *Maura* and *him* form a compound
    OBJECT of the preposition *with*.

Note the following correct form:

    The apples were divided between Tom and *me*.

In this case, *Tom* and *me* are OBJECTS of the preposition *between*.

In the following examples of pronoun difficulties, don't be fooled by the words *swimmers* and *students*. They do not affect which pronouns to use.

    We (not *Us*) swimmers are competing in the county championships.

    Mr. Gonzales took *us* (not *we*) students on a tour of the new regional high
    school.

In the first sentence, *we* is a SUBJECT of the verb *are competing*. In the second sentence, *us* is an OBJECT of the verb *took*.

Watch out for sentences that leave out a verb because it is understood.

    Dita is already as tall as *he* (not *him*).

He is the SUBJECT of the understood verb *is*. Think of the sentence as reading, "Dita is already as tall as *he is tall*."

EXERCISE 1.   In each sentence, underline the correct form of the pronoun (used as a subject) in parentheses.

1. (**We, Us**) students are late for class.

2. Maria and (**her, she**) are fond of swimming.

3. When I'm dancing, nobody else can be as happy as (**I, me**).

4. Todd and (**I, me**) went to the Lakers-Celtics game.

5. Sharon, Mike, and (**he, him**) are studying together.

EXERCISE 2.   In each sentence, underline the correct form of the pronoun (used as an object) in parentheses.

1. Mike bought shakes for him and (**I, me**).

2. Janna saw Greg and (**them, they**) on the bus.

3. The coach awarded letters to all of (**us, we**) members of the team.

4. We found our cat Max and (**she, her**) asleep on the couch.

5. Play with Sean and (**I, me**) in the band concert.

EXERCISE 3.   In each sentence, underline the correct form of the pronoun (either subject or object) in parentheses.

1. (**Her, She**) and her tennis partner will travel to Cleveland for the match.

2. Mom prepared a hot dinner for Dad and (**I, me**).

3. (**Us, We**) students are entering our sweet potato casserole in the cooking contest.

4. Devon caught sight of Lam and (**them, they**) on the bus to Lockport.

5. (**Them, They**) are applying for American citizenship as soon as possible.

6. My faithful dog and (**I, me**) climbed Mt. Washington together.

7. When it comes to precalculus, Don is as quick as (**her, she**).

8. Mr. Ortiz brought Nathan and (**her, she**) some homemade fudge.

9. The treasurer asked all of (**us, we**) club members to pay our back dues.

10. Joanna and (**them, they**) made all the sandwiches for her sister's bridal shower.

11. At the end of the recycling drive, the chairperson of the committee thanked (**us, we**) workers for our help.

12. Aaron and (**I, me**) played a strong doubles match but lost in a tiebreaker.

13. Ellen is planning a picnic for Danny and (**I, me**).

14. At the end of the school year, Sasha, Annie, and (**he, him**) were commended for academic achievement.

15. (**Us, We**) members of the National Honor Society had a special assembly.

16. Li and (**he, him**) are in the same Spanish class.

17. (**Them, They**) are the best strawberries I've ever tasted.

18. Our pen pal in Bosnia wrote a long letter to Karin and (**I, me**).

19. We saw Marisol and (**he, him**) in the stands at the baseball game.

20. (**Him and I, He and I**) went on a rafting trip on the Nantahala River.

Agreement of a Pronoun with Its Antecedent

In Part One, Lesson 9, we learned that a pronoun must agree with its antecedent in number. (The word *antecedent* comes from two Latin words meaning "going before." An antecedent is the noun that the pronoun stands for.)

Look at the following sentence:

A wolf is gentle with *its* young.

Its refers to *wolf. Wolf* is the antecedent of *its. Wolf* is singular. Therefore, *its* is singular. (Notice that the antecedent "goes before" the pronoun.)
Now look at this sentence:

Wolves are gentle with *their* young.

Their refers to *wolves. Wolves* is the antecedent of *their. Wolves* is plural. Therefore, *their* is plural.

EXERCISE 4.   In each sentence below, write a pronoun that agrees with its antecedent.

1. A girl leaving the store stumbled and dropped _____ ice cream cone.

2. Marilyn has a new dress but has not worn _____ yet.

3. Michael knows that _____ will make the team.

4. Janine likes cats, but Ariel dislikes _____.

5. The building will have _____ roof repaired.

Indefinite Pronouns

Many problems of agreement arise with the words on the following list. They are called *indefinite pronouns.* A personal pronoun that has one of these words as an antecedent must be singular.

anybody	either	neither	one
anyone	everybody	nobody	somebody
each	everyone	no one	someone

COMMON USAGE ERRORS

Note the following correct forms.

Each of the girls must bring *her* track shoes.

Each is singular. *Her* is singular.

Everybody must report to *his* or *her* adviser.

Everybody is singular. *His . . . her* with *or* is singular. Even though *everybody* "sounds" plural, it isn't. The use of *their* with *everybody*—or with any other word on the list—is incorrect in formal English.

With *either . . . or* or *neither . . . nor,* use the nearer antecedent when choosing a pronoun.

Either *Jill* or *Claire* will bring *her* records to the dance.

Jill . . . Claire is a compound subject. Since *Jill* is singular and *Claire* is also singular, the singular *her* is used.

Neither *Norm* nor his *cousins* buy *their* groceries here.

Norm is singular, but *cousins* is plural. Therefore, the plural *their* is used to agree with the nearer antecedent, *cousins*.

EXERCISE 5.   In each sentence below, underline the correct form of the possessive pronoun in parentheses.

1. Someone on the girls' field hockey team forgot (**her, their**) hockey stick.

2. No one on the swimming team gave (**his or her, their**) approval to the practice schedule.

3. An elephant forms a close bond with (**its, their**) trainer.

4. Neither Dario nor Justin had (**his, their**) purple hair for very long.

5. Everybody brought (**their, his or her**) own golf clubs.

Still another error is using a plural verb with one of the indefinite pronouns. Note these correct forms.

Everyone at the meeting *has* a stake in the decision.

Everyone is **singular.** *Has* is singular.

PROBLEMS WITH PRONOUNS   **197**

Each of the members *was* asked to vote.

Each is singular. *Was* is singular.

Neither the *twins* nor *she wants* to go to the beach this summer.

Twins is plural, but *she* is singular. The singular verb, *wants*, agrees with the nearer subject, *she*, which is also singular.

Some indefinite pronouns usually require a plural verb: *several, many, both, some, few.*

Some *were* not invited to Yolanda's party.

Many of the apples *are* still green.

Several in the stands *cheer* whenever Forenzo comes to bat.

EXERCISE 6.   Underline the correct form of the verb in parentheses.

1. Either Paul or she (**are, is**) running in Saturday's marathon.

2. Nobody in the class (**are, is**) satisfied with the test grades.

3. A few of the audience (**is, are**) leaving before the end of the play.

4. One of the rear tires (**have, has**) gone flat.

5. Both of the Baker boys (**were, was**) late to school because the bus broke down.

6. Neither Kim nor his two sisters (**is, are**) above the age of fifteen.

Possessive Pronouns

As we discovered in Lesson 9 of Part One, pronouns can cause problems in yet another area—*possessives.* You have already worked with noun possessives. With nouns, you used apostrophes to show possession.

The possessives of *personal pronouns,* however, have NO apostrophes. Note the following correct forms.

Is this *yours* or *hers*?

Those books are *theirs*, not *ours.*

Where is *its* collar?

Look carefully at the last sentence—it will help you avoid a common mistake. You have seen the word *it's*, with an apostrophe. *It's* is a contraction of *it is*. Whenever you wonder whether *its* needs an apostrophe, simply replace *its* with *it is*. If the sentence does make sense, use an apostrophe. If it doesn't make sense (as in "Where is *it is* collar?), *don't* use the apostrophe.

The possessives of *indefinite pronouns,* unlike personal pronouns, DO use apostrophes.

> *Somebody's* bookbag is on the kitchen table.
>
> *Everyone's* job is *nobody's* job.
>
> *No one's* opinion is more valued than Rebecca's.

EXERCISE 7.   In each sentence, underline the correct possessive pronoun form in parentheses.

1. The idea for improving the lunchroom is (**theirs, their's**).

2. The Joneses own the Honda; (**ours, our's**) is the Ford.

3. (**Its, It's**) starting to rain—cover the chairs.

4. Ms. Maloney is (**everybodys, everybody's**) favorite history teacher.

5. The book of Emily Dickinson's poems is (**hers, her's**).

6. Is this (**someone's, someones**) physics textbook?

7. The puppy limps because it injured (**its, it's**) paw.

8. The accident was (**nobodys, nobody's**) fault.

9. The Gerhardts spent Thanksgiving with friends of (**theirs, their's**).

10. (**Its, It's**) time to turn the light off and go to sleep.

EXERCISE 8.   In each sentence, underline the correct pronoun form in parentheses.

1. (**We, Us**) students are willing to volunteer our time in the community.

2. Jayne says that book is (**hers, her's**).

3. Go with John and (**I, me**) to the movies.

4. One of the girls (**were, was**) dismissed from the chorus.

5. Neither of the boys (**plays, play**) ice hockey.

6. (**They, Them**) are the teachers from our school.

7. Everyone on the girls' soccer team had (**her, their**) name read aloud at the awards ceremony.

8. Few students taking the test brought (**his or her, their**) own pencils.

9. Between you and (**I, me**), I thought the acting was bad.

10. Pedro and (**I, me**) liked John Grisham's latest novel.

EXERCISE 9.   Fill in the blanks with the correct pronoun.

1. Alicia was in an accident. She broke _____ leg.

2. You ordered this CD and paid for it. Take it. It is _____.

3. Jon and I are neighbors. _____ lives next door to me.

4. Linda and Safiya are our friends. We like _____ very much.

5. The ball came right to you, but your bat could not connect with _____.

6. Meredith gave Matt the book. _____ had bought it especially for _____.

7. One of the boys played in every game of the tournament. _____ was exhausted.

8. The coach and the team prepared for the game. _____ still lost.

9. Did you know the last answer? _____ was easy, wasn't it?

10. My older sister made the last payment on her car. Now it belongs to _____.

Lesson 25 Problems with Punctuation

A complete list of punctuation rules would fill a book. Fortunately, you don't have to learn them all. Mastery of a few basic rules will help you avoid most of the pitfalls in punctuating sentences. The following review covers the main points.

End Punctuation

Every sentence ends with a *period*, a *question mark*, or an *exclamation point*.

STATEMENT:	A Pekingese has a longer life expectancy than a Saint Bernard.
COMMAND:	Read the instructions on how to set up your printer.
POLITE REQUEST:	Would you please lock up before you leave for the day.
QUESTION:	Have you ever visited Acadia National Park?
STRONG FEELING:	What a great time we had at Disney World!

EXERCISE 1.   Copy these sentences, writing the proper end punctuation marks.

1. Where did you put the hammer

   _____

2. Please pass the butter

   _____

3. How gorgeous that sunset is

   _____

4. Why didn't you mow the lawn

   _____

5. The word *paper* comes from the Egyptian word for papyrus

   _____

The period is also used after *abbreviations* and *most initials*.

Dr. R. J. Lowenherz   P.M.   Jr.   R.S.V.P.

The Comma

Of the comma's many uses, three important ones you should review are use of commas in a series; use of commas to set off interrupting words and expressions; and use of commas in letters, dates, and addresses.

Commas in a Series

Use a comma to separate *items in a series*.

> Last summer we hiked, swam, golfed, and played softball.
>
> My brother collects stamps, coins, and baseball cards.
>
> I looked frantically looked for the tickets on the desk, in the desk drawer, and on the dresser.

Some writers omit the comma before the *and*. This can be confusing in some sentences, however. The safest practice is to include the final comma in all such sentences.

When more than one adjective precedes a noun, use a comma for a *pause*.

> The gloomy, isolated mansion stood at the edge of a cliff. (Pause after *gloomy*.)
>
> Oliver was a lively young dog. (No pause.)

Commas to Set Off Interrupters

Use a pair of commas to enclose most *interrupting words or expressions*.

> Our Mr. Pooch, like most beagles, is a friendly dog.
>
> Siamese cats, on the other hand, are more reserved.
>
> Tallahassee, not Miami, is the capital of Florida.
>
> I'm surprised, Tessa, that you believe his story.
>
> She admitted that, yes, she could see his point of view.
>
> The route through Evansville is, according to Jack, the best route to Melissa's house.
>
> The old car, rusted and dented, was not worth fixing.

When an interrupter comes at the beginning or at the end of a sentence, only one comma is needed.

> Like most beagles, our Mr. Pooch is a friendly dog.
>
> On the other hand, Siamese cats are more reserved.

The capital of Florida is Tallahassee, not Miami.

I'm surprised that you believe his story, Tessa.

Yes, I admit that I can see your point of view.

Paul disagrees, however.

Rusted and dented, the old car was not worth fixing.

Use a comma to enclose most appositives (see Lesson 19, page 136). An **appositive** explains the noun or pronoun it follows. It is most commonly a noun.

Songhay, an African *kingdom* in the late 1400s, was larger than Western Europe.

The Antarctic waters, *fertilizer* for the rest of the world, help support life in the other oceans.

Adjectives sometimes appear in the appositive position.

The old prison, *grim* and *foreboding*, would be torn down in a few months.

Spiders, *unpopular* but *essential*, destroy a hundred times their number in insects.

Use commas to enclose appositives preceded by *or.*

The avocado, or *alligator pear*, was first cultivated by the Aztecs.

EXERCISE 2.   Copy these sentences, adding all needed punctuation. Note that end punctuation must be added, too.

1. Saturday was a dark cold dreary day

   _____

   _____

2. The firefly or lightning bug flashes light in the summer night sky.

   _____

   _____

3. No I strongly object to your remarks

   _____

   _____

4. Did you ever find your missing notebook Tammy

   _____

   _____

5. Blue not red is Sara's favorite color

_____

_____

6. Elizabeth however prefers green especially light green

_____

_____

7. Tej is a fine swimmer diver golfer and soccer player

_____

_____

8. Are you aware that George Washington our first President served two terms

_____

_____

9. William Henry Harrison on the other hand served only a month

_____

_____

10. Corn on the cob my favorite vegetable should not be overcooked.

_____

_____

11. The coffee tree a native of Africa still grows wild in Ethiopia and Liberia

_____

_____

12. This summer we hiked in Pisgah National Forest ate lunch by waterfalls and enjoyed views from mountaintops

_____

_____

13. I'm grateful to you Ethan and Becky for taping that program we wanted to see

_____

_____

14. The sassafras unlike most trees has three different and distinct leaf patterns

_____

_____

15. Sandra please hand me that hammer

_____

_____

16. On our trip we visited Banff Lake Louise and Jasper

_____

_____

17. The mountain range stark and majestic was outlined against the sky

_____

_____

18. Where did you put the laundry detergent Ronnie

_____

_____

19. Alfred Nobel the inventor of dynamite also invented plywood

_____

_____

20. Freezing temperatures not wind are threatening the orange crop

_____

_____

Commas in Letters, Dates, and Addresses

1. When dates and addresses occur within sentences, you punctuate them as in the following examples.

   Write to Megan Acieri, 908 Beechwood Drive, Hendersonville, NC 28739.
   (Note that there is no comma between the name of the state and the ZIP code.)

   Mr. Blakiston was born on June 19, 1963, in Chicago, Illinois.
   (Note that there is a comma after the year as well as in front of it.)

2. When dates and addresses appear in the heading or the inside address of a letter, you punctuate them like this:

   33 Barrett Street
   Elmira, NY 14904
   August 22, 2003

   Mr. Stephen Dorney
   La Bravura Drive
   Beverly Hills, CA 90213

The U.S. Postal Service recommends two-letter state abbreviations for addressing letters. These abbreviations have no periods (*NY*, not *N.Y.*), and they often differ from traditional abbreviations (*CA*, not *Cal.* or *Calif.*). If you are unsure of the two-letter abbreviation, write out the state or U.S. possession name. A list of official postal abbreviations follows.

State/Possession	*Abbreviation*
Alabama	AL
Alaska	AK
American Samoa	AS
Arizona	AZ
Arkansas	AR
California	CA
Colorado	CO
Connecticut	CT
Delaware	DE
District of Columbia	DC
Federated States of Micronesia	FM
Florida	FL
Georgia	GA
Guam	GU
Hawaii	HI
Idaho	ID
Illinois	IL
Indiana	IN
Iowa	IA
Kansas	KS
Kentucky	KY
Louisiana	LA
Maine	ME
Marshall Islands	MH
Maryland	MD
Massachusetts	MA
Michigan	MI
Minnesota	MN
Mississippi	MS

Missouri	MO
Montana	MT
Nebraska	NE
Nevada	NV
New Hampshire	NH
New Jersey	NJ
New Mexico	NM
New York	NY
North Carolina	NC
North Dakota	ND
Northern Mariana Islands	MP
Ohio	OH
Oklahoma	OK
Oregon	OR
Palau	PW
Pennsylvania	PA
Puerto Rico	PR
Rhode Island	RI
South Carolina	SC
South Dakota	SD
Tennessee	TN
Texas	TX
Utah	UT
Vermont	VT
Virgin Islands	VI
Virginia	VA
Washington	WA
West Virginia	WV
Wisconsin	WI
Wyoming	WY

3. Use a comma after the salutation (*Dear* _____,) of a friendly letter and the complimentary close (*Sincerely, Regards, Best wishes,* and so on) of all letters.

Dear Carole,   Sincerely,
Dear Uncle Frank,   Very truly yours,

4. Use a colon after the salutation of a business letter.

Gentlemen: Dear Ms. Valenzuela:

EXERCISE 3.   Copy these sentences, adding all needed punctuation. Note that end punctuation must also be added.

1. The American Heart Association is located at 2524 Farragut Drive Suite A Springfield IL 62704

    _____

    _____

2. Was it April 25 1990 when the Hubble Space Telescope was launched

    _____

    _____

3. The United Negro College Fund has offices at 2750 Prosperity Ave Fairfax VA 22031

    _____

    _____

4. Write to Yellowstone National Park P.O. Box 168 WY 82190-0168

    _____

    _____

5. John Adams and Thomas Jefferson died on July 4 1826 exactly fifty years after signing the Declaration of Independence

    _____

    _____

6. On May 5 1961 Alan B Shepard Jr became the first American in space

    _____

    _____

7. My brother lives at 15 Dogwood Circle Boynton Beach FL 33462

    _____

    _____

8. William Jefferson Clinton was born on August 19 1946 and became President of the United States at the age of 46

    _____

    _____

9. Sandra ordered a jacket from L. L. Bean Inc Freeport ME 04033-0001

_____

_____

10. Neil Armstrong US astronaut first walked on the moon July 20 1969

_____

_____

Quotation Marks

A direct quotation shows the speaker's exact words. An indirect quotation does not.

DIRECT QUOTATION: Dad said, "You can work at the ice cream stand this summer." (Quotation marks needed)

INDIRECT QUOTATION: Dad said that I can work at the ice cream stand this summer. (No quotation marks needed)

Quotation marks always go in pairs. If you have opening quotation marks, you must have closing quotation marks.

Ellen said, "I'm taking the school bus home."

"I'm taking the school bus home," Ellen said.

"When do you leave?" asked Carlos.

Carlos asked, "When do you leave?"

"I hope," said Fiona, "that you remember to take your science book home."

"When do we eat?" William asked. "I'm hungry."

Did William say, "I'm hungry"?
(The question mark goes outside the closing quotation marks because the entire sentence is a question.)

"I never saw a snow leopard before," Maureen said. "Did you?"

EXERCISE 4. Copy the following sentences. Add all needed punctuation.

1. Let's go fishing in Murray Creek suggested Anna

_____

_____

2. Rob replied I promised Dad I'd trim the hedge

_____

_____

3. What book did you choose for a report asked Mr. Lopez

_____

_____

4. That was a great play yelled Paul

_____

_____

5. It was the first time said Dara that I've thrown the ball that far

_____

_____

6. How did ragtime music start asked Andrew

_____

_____

7. The coach stopped Chan and asked are you trying out for the team

_____

_____

8. Work is the best method devised for killing time said William Feather

_____

_____

9. Education is what remains said Lord Halifax when we have forgotten all that we have been taught

_____

_____

10. I must follow the people said Benjamin Disraeli am I not their leader

_____

_____

Punctuating Titles

In general, use quotation marks around the titles of short works—a short story, an essay, a song, a magazine article, or the chapter of a book. Underline the titles of longer works—a book, a film, a magazine, or a newspaper. (In printed material, underlined words appear in *italics*.) Here are some examples:

"The Keeper of the Keys" is the title of a chapter in *Harry Potter and the Sorcerer's Stone* by J.K. Rowling.

"Sweet Virginia" is my mother's favorite song from the Rolling Stones' album *Exile on Main Street.*

I've seen the movie *Chicago* at least five times.

TV Guide is one of the most successful magazines ever published.

The *Courier-Post* serves southern New Jersey.
(Be careful to capitalize the exact name of the newspaper. Usually *the* is not capitalized as part of the name, but in *The New York Times* it is. Sometimes the name of the city is part of the name of the paper, as in the *Chicago Sun-Times,* and sometimes it isn't.)

EXERCISE 5.   Copy the following sentences. Punctuate each correctly.

1. The Red Badge of Courage is the book I have decided to read for my book report

_____

_____

2. The newspaper Newsday has many readers, but not as many as the Times

_____

_____

3. Did you see Pirates of the Caribbean

_____

_____

4. She wrote a story called After Dark which was published in Seventeen magazine

_____

_____

5. Hey, Jude is my aunt's favorite Beatles tune

_____

_____

EXERCISE 6.   Copy these sentences, adding all needed punctuation.

1. Did you go to the Dolphins games asked Mr. Gomez

_____

_____

2. Caroline went to see Terminator 3: Rise of the Machines in Joplin Missouri

_____

_____

3. Jillian bought new shoes sweaters skirts and jeans

_____

_____

4. I wonder said Alyssa where I put my new sunglasses

_____

_____

5. No I want you to do your homework first said her mother

_____

_____

6. James said that his new address would be 21330 Fronthill Avenue Torrance CA 90505

_____

_____

7. My brother was born October 22 1995 which was a Sunday

_____

_____

8. Sometimes it is confusing said Mr. Thomas but the New York Giants play their home games in New Jersey

_____

_____

9. I'm surprised Rick that you did not bring your friend

_____

_____

10. I read an article called Without Fear in Time magazine

_____

_____

EXERCISE 7. For the underlined part of each of the following sentences, there are four suggested answers. Write the letter of the correct answer on the line at the right.

1. <u>Oh its</u> a long time until the end of the movie.

   (*a*) Correct as is   (*c*) Oh, its'

   (*b*) Oh, its   (*d*) Oh, it's   1. _____

2. "Will you let me use the <u>car" Jim asked?</u>

    (*a*) Correct as is   (*c*) car?" Jim asked.

    (*b*) car," Jim asked?   (*d*) car, Jim asked.   2. _____

3. Did you <u>read A Tale of Two Cities.</u>

    (*a*) Correct as is   (*c*) read, "A Tale of Two Cities"

    (*b*) read *A Tale of Two Cities*?   (*d*) read A Tale of Two Cities?   3. _____

4. It was <u>June 12, 2003 when</u> we went on the trip.

    (*a*) Correct as is   (*c*) June 12, 2003, when

    (*b*) June 12 2003 when   (*d*) June, 12, 2003, when   4. _____

5. <u>What said Stephanie did</u> you mean by that remark?"

    (*a*) Correct as is   (*c*) "What," said Stephanie, "did

    (*b*) "What," said Stephanie "did   (*d*) What said, Stephanie, Did   5. _____

Lesson 26 Problems with Capitalization

The following review summarizes the important rules of capitalization.

In Letters

Capitalize the first word and all nouns in the *salutation.*

Dear James,   Dear Mr. Patterson:

Dear Aunt Jane,   Dear Miss McCloud:

Capitalize only the first word in the *complimentary close.*

Your friend,   Very truly yours,

Your niece,   Cordially yours,

In Quotations

A *direct quotation* begins with a capital letter.

Edgar Allan Poe wrote, "Quoth the Raven, 'Nevermore.'"

When a one-sentence quotation is interrupted, however, the second part does not start with a capital.

"Does anyone," Bethany asked, "know where my ice skates are?"

See Lesson 25, pages 209–211, for other examples of capitalizating quotations.

First Words

Capitalize the first word of a complete sentence, the comments of each new speaker in conversation, and each line of poetry or verse.

SENTENCE: The antelope survives on dry plains.

CONVERSATION: "You begin to comprehend me, do you?" cried he, turning towards her.

"**O**h! yes—I understand you perfectly."

"**I** wish I might take this for a compliment; but to be so easily seen through I am afraid is pitiful."

—from Jane Austen's *Pride and Prejudice*

POETRY: **T**he pedigree of honey
       Does not concern the bee;
    A clover, any time, to him
       Is aristocracy.

—Emily Dickinson

Proper Nouns and Proper Adjectives

Capitalize *proper nouns,* their *abbreviations,* and *proper adjectives* derived from proper nouns.

PROPER NOUN: **New Mexico**

ABBREVIATION: **N.M.** (or NM, the postal abbreviation)

PROPER ADJECTIVE: **New Mexican** (as in *New Mexican* art)

EXERCISE 1.

A. Copy the following, adding needed capitals.

1. dear mr. keane: _____

2. your friend,   _____

3. dear stefan,   _____

4. sincerely yours,   _____

5. dear mr. thomas: _____

6. yours very truly,   _____

B. Copy the following, and capitalize each sentence correctly.

1. a local anchorperson used to end her evening broadcasts by saying, "have a good day tomorrow."

_____

_____

2. "do you know," asked the teacher, "who serves as the secretary of state?"

_____

_____

3. he said, with a smile on his face, "look at my grades."

_____

_____

C. Correctly capitalize the following conversation.

"where were you born?" asked the interviewer.
mariel said, "i was born in columbus, ohio."
"when did you move to north carolina?"
"in 2002, when my father accepted his new job here."

_____

_____

_____

_____

EXERCISE 2. Copy the following, and capitalize each sentence correctly.

1. susie began her letter, "dear aunt olivia."

_____

_____

2. mark twain said, "if you tell the truth, you don't have to remember anything."

_____

_____

3. "why don't you take art as an elective next year?" suggested mrs. esposito.

_____

_____

4. "you know," said the guidance counseler, "you really should apply for early decision."

_____

_____

5. will rogers said, "don't let yesterday use up too much of today."

_____

_____

Here are some specific kinds of proper nouns, with examples, that require capital letters.

Names of particular persons, real or imaginary

> **Linda, Jeremy, Shania Twain, Ben Affleck, Sandra Day O'Connor, James Bond, Frodo Baggins**

Geographical names

> **Australia, New Jersey, Palm Beach County, Yosemite National Park, Fifth Avenue**

Titles of organizations, companies, and buildings

> **Kiwanis Club, National Audubon Society, Ford Motor Company, Riverside Cathedral**

Political parties, nations, government bodies

> **Republican, Democrat, France, Czech Republic, Zimbabwe, Senate, Department of the Interior**

Titles of persons showing office, rank, profession

> **President Roosevelt, General Marshall, Dr. Reed, Professor Hutchinson**

Names of planets, satellites, stars, and constellations

> **Jupiter, Ganymede, Sirius, the Big Dipper**
> (*Note:* The words *sun, earth,* and *moon* are often not capitalized.)

Names of days of the week, months, holidays

> **Thursday, March, Independence Day**
> (*Note:* The names of the seasons are not capitalized.)

Titles

> ***Gone with the Wind, Better Homes and Gardens,* "The Night the Ghost Got In"**
> (*Note:* Articles—*a, an, the*—prepositions, and conjunctions are not capitalized unless they occur at the beginning or end of a title.)

Brand names

> **Campbell's soups, Pepperidge Farm bread, Green Giant broccoli**

Names referring to God, the Bible, or religions

> **the Almighty, Exodus, the Old Testament, Christianity, Hinduism, Buddhism, Islam, the Torah**

There are three kinds of items that require extra thought if you are to capitalize them correctly.

Sections of the country

the **S**outheast, the **N**orthwest, the **S**outhwest

Do *not* capitalize these words if they are merely compass points:

Philadelphia lies southwest of New York City.

Family relationships

Father, **C**ousin **G**ene, **A**unt **G**loria, **G**randpa

Do *not* capitalize these family titles unless they are used before a name (**U**ncle **S**id) or as a name (Hi, **M**om):

My mom, sister, cousin, and aunt visited Duke Gardens.

School subjects: languages and numbered courses

English, **F**rench, **S**panish, **G**erman, **M**echanical **D**rawing 2, **S**ocial **S**tudies 3, **M**athematics 4

Do *not* capitalize the names of unnumbered courses except for languages:

I'm taking mechanical drawing, social studies, mathematics, and **G**erman in the fall.

EXERCISE 3. Draw a circle around each letter that should be capitalized.

1. my uncle in london

2. the republican candidate

3. english and history

4. the planet saturn

5. fourth of july holiday

6. john jay high school

7. *lord of the rings: return of the king*

8. grandma and aunt louise

9. in the southwest near phoenix

10. fire island national seashore

EXERCISE 4.

A. Copy these sentences, adding needed capitals.

1. mayor chang spoke at the meeting of the rotary club.

   _____

   _____

2. the blue ridge parkway winds through some of the most beautiful mountain scenery in the east.

   _____

   _____

3. my sister has already taken spanish and french in high school.

   _____

   _____

4. a ford assembly plant is being built at the corner of spring street and linden boulevard.

   _____

   _____

5. the only continent my uncle hasn't visited is antarctica.

   _____

   _____

6. the empire state building is still a major tourist attraction in new york city.

   _____

   _____

7. the department of agriculture oversees our national forests.

   _____

   _____

8. i saw venus and jupiter in the sky at twilight on labor day.

   _____

   _____

9. the first two books of the old testament are genesis and exodus.

   _____

   _____

10. my cousin, major andrea langer, has just returned from a tour of duty in the northwest.

_____

_____

B. Copy the following poem, adding needed capitals.

        but do not let us quarrel any more,
        no, my lucrezia; bear with me for once:
        sit down and all shall happen as you wish.
        you turn your face, but does it bring your heart?
                —Robert Browning, "Andrea del Sarto"

Lesson 27 Problems with Spelling

You are more likely to misspell common words than uncommon ones. That happens because you probably look up the spellings of hard words but assume that you know how to spell the easy ones.

Frequently Misspelled Words

The commonly used words in the following list are among the most frequently misspelled. Review them and master them.

ache	broccoli	excitement	meant
accommodate	built	exhilarate	minute
accumulate	business	experience	necessary
acquaint	captain	feasible	noticeable
across	certain	foreign	occasion
agreeable	character	friend	occurred
a lot (*not* alot)	coming	grammar	occurrence
all right (*not* alright)	committee	handkerchief	often
almost	correspondence	having	omitted
always	cough	heard	once
among	course	hospital	piece
another	describe	immediately	pleasant
appreciate	disappear	indispensable	principal [school]
asked	disappoint	inoculate	privilege
athletic	doctor	instead	probably
beautiful	doesn't	irresistible	realize
before	dropped	knew	really
believe	embarrass	knowledge	receive
benefit	enough	library	recommend
boundary	every	lightning	resistance
break	exception	maintenance	rhythm
			continued

says	straight	though	until
scene	studying	thought	weird
secretary	success	threw	which
separate	supersede	together	woman
since	surely	toward	writing
speech	surprise		

EXERCISE 1.   In each sentence below, there is a partially spelled word. Write the complete word in the space at the right.

1. When Jan won the contest, there was a lot of
   exci_____ment at our house.   _____

2. It is not **nec_____ry** to answer my letter.   _____

3. The teacher appointed a **com_____tee** to
   study the problem.   _____

4. I'll meet you in the **lib_____y.**   _____

5. Jack is having a **su_____rise** party for Gina.   _____

6. The new rules will **ben_____it** everyone in
   the class.   _____

7. **Al_____ight,** I'll help with the refreshments
   at the party.   _____

8. Mr. Parker wants to **rec_____ve** those reports now,
   not tomorrow.   _____

9. I think my most **emba_____ing** moment was
   when I forgot my lines in the junior play.   _____

10. I'm not **cert_____n,** but I think Jordan will
    take Lisa to the dance.   _____

11. Is there a difference between **kno_____ge** and
    wisdom?   _____

12. Pat has scholastic as well as **ath_____tic** skills.   _____

13. The **princip_____** of our school once ran in the
    Olympics.   _____

14. My mom says that dad is her best **fr_____nd.**   _____

15. I hope my cold **dis_____p_____ears** before the class trip.

    _____

16. I've been **stud_____ng** for the test since march.

    _____

17. Does every rule have an **ex_____ption?**

    _____

18. The **capt_____n** of the soccer team can run 100 yards in 10 seconds.

    _____

19. Come to the play; don't **dis_____point** us.

    _____

20. My graduation will be an important **oc_____sion.**

    _____

Words Often Confused

In addition to words that are tricky to spell, English also has its share of words that are easily—and often—confused. Note the correct spelling of the words in boldface type.

I'll **accept** every package **except** the one with the torn wrapping.

We looked at old pictures. **Then** Peter was taller **than** Matthew.

She's **too** late **to** enter the race.

Because of all the trees surrounding our house, it is **quite quiet.**

Your earring is **loose.** Don't **lose** it.

Whether we go or not depends on the **weather.**

It's time to give the cat **its** lunch.

You're leading **your** opponent in the election.

They're going **there** with **their** hopes high.

Where can I **wear** this vintage dress I found in the attic?

EXERCISE 2.　　In each sentence, underline the correct spelling.

1. I think Val's report was (**quiet, quite**) interesting.

2. (**Their, There**) is no reason for becoming discouraged.

3. (**Wear, Where**) did you put the ice skates?

4. I hope I didn't (**loose, lose**) my combination lock. I can't find it anywhere.

5. Please (**accept, except**) our congratulations for the honor you have won.

6. That lively spaniel is older (**than, then**) that weary-looking golden retriever.

7. I don't know (**weather, whether**) I'll be able to finish my report in time.

8. Maura was glad to learn that (**your, you're**) coming to the basketball game.

9. Sometimes Bazyli can be just (**to, too**) relaxed.

10. (**It's, Its**) your move.

11. (**Its, It's**) (**to, too**) early to leave for the party.

12. Everyone in the class is shorter (**than, then**) Pedro (**accept, except**) Clark.

13. (**Weather, Whether**) or not my parents buy the new house depends on how (**quiet, quite**) the neighborhood is.

14. (**Your, You're**) lucky you didn't (**loose, lose**) the bracelet you like so much.

15. They can do what they want; it's (**there, their**) money.

Seven Helpful Spelling Rules

These following simple rules can help you to spell a great many words correctly.

1. **Ei, Ie.** Put **i** before **e** except after **c**, or when sounded like **a** as in *neighbor* and *weigh*.

i before **e**:	bel**ie**ve, ch**ie**f, n**ie**ce, f**ie**ld, sh**ie**ld
except after **c**:	**cei**ling, re**cei**ve, de**cei**t, con**cei**t, per**cei**ve
sounded like **a**:	w**ei**ght, v**ei**l, v**ei**n, r**ei**gn, r**ei**n
Exceptions:	for**ei**gner, l**ei**sure, **ei**ther, n**ei**ther, h**ei**ght

EXERCISE 3. Fill in the missing letters, and write the complete word at the right.

1. Please answer **br____fly.** _____

2. How much do the potatoes **w____gh?** _____

3. Dana is your **n____ghbor.** _____

4. What is your **h____ght?** _____

5. We installed a **c____ling** fan. _____

6. The **r_____gn** of Queen Victoria was one of
the longest in history.   _____

7. **N_____ther** answer is correct.   _____

8. May I have a **p_____ce** of cherry pie?   _____

9. Did you **rec_____ve** my card from Yellowstone? _____

10. A person's use of **l_____sure** is a key to his or
her character.   _____

   2. Ly. Keep the original **l** when adding **ly** to a word ending in **l**.

   actua**lly**, beautifu**lly**, cheerfu**lly**, fina**lly**, rea**lly**

EXERCISE 4.   Fill in the missing letters, and write the complete word at the right.

1. Look **carefu_____y** before crossing the street.   _____

2. Lena strolled **casua_____y** through the mall.   _____

3. Attendance was **unusua_____y** large today.   _____

4. Aunt Leila greeted her guests **cordia_____y.**   _____

5. That mischievous child tossed my book into the lake
intentiona_____y.   _____

6. Our car was **fu_____y** packed.   _____

7. I tripped **accidenta_____y.**   _____

8. We accepted the advice **gratefu_____y.**   _____

9. I couldn't believe we had **actua_____y** arrived.   _____

10. Jeff cleaned up the messy kitchen **cheerful_____y.** _____

   3. Final E Before Vowel. Drop silent **e** before a suffix beginning with a vowel.

   admir~~e~~able, argu~~e~~ing, larg~~e~~est, enclos~~e~~ing, scarc~~e~~ity

EXERCISE 5.   Fill in the missing letters, and write the complete word at the right.

1. **Advers_____ty** is no stranger to some unfortunate
people.   _____

2. This brand of detergent made my white shirt look even **whit____r.**

_____

3. The network is **experienc____g** technical difficulties.

_____

4. He plays wide **receiv____r** on the team.

_____

5. Time off from school is very **desir____ble.**

_____

6. The players were **argu____g** over the umpire's decision.

_____

7. Max was **practic____g** his guitar.

_____

8. Kathryn has an **admir____le** record in French.

_____

9. Mark's story is **unbeliev____le.**

_____

10. Our cat kept **interfer____g** with my homework.

_____

4. Final E Before Consonant. Keep final silent **e** before a suffix beginning with a consonant.

amaz**e**ment, aton**e**ment, hop**e**ful, fortunat**e**ly, us**e**ful

Exceptions: acknowledgment, argument, awful, duly, judgment, ninth, truly, wholly

EXERCISE 6.   Fill in the missing letters, and write the complete word at the right.

1. There was a lot of **excit____ment** about the game.

_____

2. Evan is **hop____lessly** behind in his schoolwork; but now that he is feeling better, he expects to catch up.

_____

3. She was told to be very **car____ful** with the car.

_____

4. **Saf____ty** first!

_____

5. Lucinda looks **lov____ly** in her new gown.

_____

6. **Nin____een** planes were ahead of us on the runway.

_____

7. Failing to recycle is **wast____ul.**

_____

8. It's best to study in **peac____ul** surroundings.

_____

9. Justine **car____ully** opened the package.

_____

10. **Fortunat_____y** I had an extra set of keys.   _____

    5. Final Y. If final **y** is preceded by a consonant, change **y** to **i** when you add a suffix.

        ap**ply** + ed = applied (**Y** changed to **i**.)

        friend**ly** + er = friendlier

        noi**sy** + est = noisiest

    But notice the following forms:

        apply + ing = applying
            (**Y** does not change to **i** if the suffix begins with **i**.)

        play + er = player
            (**Y** does not change to **i** if **y** is preceded by a vowel.)

EXERCISE 7.   Fill in the missing letters, and write the complete word at the right.

1. The two girls **hurr_____d** home after school.   _____

2. The paint is **dr_____ng** very fast.   _____

3. This holiday, my mother is **bus_____er** than ever.   _____

4. The school secretary has **suppl____** us with paper.   _____

5. The company was slow in **repl_____ng** to my sister's
letter.   _____

6. I **spra_____ed** water on the dirty window.   _____

7. Nathan **accompan_____d** Aunt Lucy to the airport.   _____

8. Jermaine has never been **happ_____r**.   _____

9. Marci **stud____d** all night.   _____

10. After passing through security, we **carr____d** our hand
luggage to the plane.   _____

    6. Doubling Final Consonant—One-Syllable Words. Note the following correct
forms. Each final consonant is preceded by a single vowel.

        bat + er = ba**tt**er
            (The final consonant, **t**, is doubled.)

        big + est = bi**gg**est

drop + ing = dro**pp**ing

grin + ed = gri**nn**ed

What happens when the final consonant is preceded by more than one vowel?

beat + en = bea**t**en
    (The final consonant, **t**, is not doubled.)

sail + ed = sai**l**ed

dream + er = drea**m**er

fool + ish = foo**l**ish

foam + ing = foa**m**ing

EXERCISE 8.   Fill in the missing letters, and write the complete word at the right.

1. The lost puppy was **roa____ing** the street.   _____

2. Jessica was the last **swi____er** to reach the shore.   _____

3. She was **pla_____ing** to go to the mall.   _____

4. The rain **sto_____ed** and the sun shone again.   _____

5. Elizabeth **fail_____d** to return my call.   _____

6. The receiver **drop_____d** the ball in the end zone.   _____

7. Our neighbor **help_____d** us with the painting.   _____

8. Is that package **wrap_____d** well?   _____

9. Without water, the flowers **droop_____d.**   _____

10. The wood under the front porch steps had **rot_____d.**   _____

7. **Doubling Final Consonant—Words of More Than One Syllable.** If a word has more than one syllable and the accent is on the last syllable, the same rule applies as for a one-syllable word.

commit + ed = commi**tt**ed
    (The accent is on the last syllable **t** is doubled.)

control + ing = contro**ll**ing

equip + ed = equi**pp**ed

propel + er = prope**ll**er

refer + ed = refe**rr**ed

What happens if the word is not accented on the last syllable?

refer + ence = reference
   (The accent is not on **er**; **r** is not doubled.)

EXERCISE 9. Fill in the missing letters, and write the complete word at the right.

1. Don **prefe_____ed** another doctor. _____

2. The accident was **regre_____able.** _____

3. Who **benefi_____ed** from the donation? _____

4. The movie **diffe_____ed** from the book. _____

5. She is **excel_____ing** in music. _____

6. **Control_____ng** a spirited horse isn't easy. _____

7. Those **swim_____rs** are trying out for the Olympic team. _____

8. Marcus **offer_____d** to run first in the half-mile relay. _____

9. For trekking in Nepal, a hiker must be well **equip_____d.** _____

10. Nadine has always **excel_____d** in craft work. _____

EXERCISE 10. In this exercise, apply all the spelling rules you have learned. Fill in the missing letters in the sentences below.

1. Ana brought me a colorful embroidered **handkerch_____f** from Mexico.

2. We **usu_____y** visit my grandmother once a month.

3. That tower is **interfe_____ng** with television reception.

4. There were **nin_____een** hikers on our last outing.

5. We have **occup_____ed** our new house for three months now.

6. The cast and crew are **plan_____ng** a post-performance party.

7. Martina was a good piano player, but Patrice **excel_____d** on the violin.

8. The next **meet_____g** of the class officers will be held next Tuesday.

9. In *Othello,* Iago **dec_____ves** his trusting friend.

10. Have you ever **tr_____ed** to play badminton?

11. When the rookie **fina_____y** hit a home run, the spectators gave him a standing ovation.

12. I am **enclos_____ng** a photograph.

13. Computers are **us_____ful,** to say the least!

14. Rhonda is **friend_____r** than Samantha.

15. Mark is the next **ba_____er** at the plate.

Contractions

As you may remember from Part One, Lessons 3 and 9, a ***contraction*** is a combination of two words with one or more letters omitted. Insert an apostrophe where one or more letters are left out in a word. In writing contractions, don't add a letter and don't change the letters around. Here is an exercise to reinforce your knowledge.

EXERCISE 11.   Write the correct contraction for each word group.

1. that + is   _____

2. you + have _____

3. did + not   _____

4. it + is   _____

5. does + not _____

6. has + not   _____

7. we + will   _____

8. do + not   _____

9. I + am   _____

10. they + are   _____

Part **Four** *Basic Paragraph Composition*

Just as words form sentences, so sentences form paragraphs. In Part Two, we learned that good sentences are concise, clear, unified, varied, and interesting. A good paragraph has all these qualities, too. Yet with paragraphs, we are thinking in "bigger" terms—how sentences relate to one another rather than how words do. Paragraphs themselves are the building blocks for essays, term papers, book reports, business letters, and so on. Mastering the techniques of effective paragraph composition, then, will go a long way toward ensuring your success in the critical skill of essay writing.

The lessons in Part Four show you ways to create paragraphs that will stay on track and keep your readers reading.

Lesson 28 The Paragraph

A *paragraph* is a group of sentences telling about one topic.

For example, read the following two paragraphs about Lance Armstrong:

From an early age, Lance Armstrong demonstrated superior athletic ability and a competitive streak. These qualities helped him win the Kids Triathlon at age 13 and, at age 16, become a professional triathlete. The cycling part of the triathlon became his focus, and he devoted his life to professional cycling. In that sport he has excelled as national and world champion, as Olympian, and as record-tying five-time winner of the Tour de France. He is surely one of the all-time great cyclists.

His path, however, has not been without obstacles and pain. In October 1996, he discovered that he had testicular cancer that had advanced and spread to his brain and lungs. The determination that had carried him through win after win in cycling now kicked in to help him combat the deadly disease. And combat he did. After surgery and chemotherapy, Lance became a cancer survivor. Profoundly affected by his battle for life, he dedicated himself to becoming a spokesperson for cancer awareness and survivorship.

Question: Why does a new paragraph begin with the sentence "His path, however, has not been without obstacles and pain"?

Answer: This is a new topic.

The first paragraph deals with Lance's achievement in cycling. All sentences in this paragraph deal with this topic.

The second paragraph moves on to another topic: Lance's battle with and victory over cancer. All sentences in this paragraph deal with this topic.

Note that the beginning of a paragraph is *indented;* that is, the first word is moved a short space to the right of the margin.

Summary: **A *paragraph* is a group of sentences telling about one topic. When you come to a new topic, begin a new paragraph. Remember to indent when you start a paragraph.**

A Note About Paragraph Length

How long should a paragraph be? Quite simply, it should be as long as it needs to be. A paragraph that is developing a topic does not consist of a predetermined number of sentences. However, very long paragraphs (say, a page long) often seem forbidding to the reader. Very short ones—one or two sentences—may be used, but only with care. Sometimes the one-sentence paragraph can make a point dramatically. A series of one-sentence paragraphs, though, makes your writing disjointed and leaves the reader with the impression that you have not developed your subject.

EXERCISE. Write a two-paragraph composition beginning with the words *The most stressful day that I remember . . .*

It is a good idea to write about something you have actually lived through. Here are examples:

The day I fell from a ladder	The day our car was stolen
The day we moved from Ridgefield	The day I started high school

Suggestions for the First Paragraph

1. Tell what day it was (The day I fell from a ladder). Give the exact date, if possible. Say how old you were at the time.
2. Topic of the first paragraph: *the day of the accident.*

Suggestions for the Second Paragraph

1. Give further *details* (information). For example, if you are writing about the day you fell from a ladder, tell how the accident happened and how badly you were hurt.
2. Topic of the second paragraph: *details of the accident.*

The following model composition shows one way of writing the two paragraphs.

Model Composition

The most stressful day that I remember is the day I fell from a ladder. It was July 4, 2000. I was almost thirteen at the time.

My father, who was working in the attic over our garage, had just asked me to hand him a piece of lumber. As I climbed up the ladder to give it to him, the ladder swayed and I fell on my back against the concrete floor. Immediately, I was in pain and shock. The breath had been knocked out of me. As I was being rushed to the hospital, I kept thinking I might never be able to walk again. To my relief, it turned out that there was no fracture, but my back was sore for a couple of days.

Now write your two-paragraph composition.

_____

_____

_____

_____

_____

_____

_____

_____

_____

_____

_____

_____

_____

_____

Lesson 29 Unity in the Paragraph

The key to effective paragraph writing is *unity*.

Question 1: What is unity?

Answer: Unity comes from the Latin word *unus,* meaning "one." **Unity means "oneness."**

A paragraph has *unity* if it deals with *one* main topic and all its sentences stick to that topic—and contribute something to it.

Suppose the first paragraph about Lance Armstrong had been written this way:

> From an early age, Lance Armstrong demonstrated superior athletic ability and a competitive streak. These qualities helped him win the Kids Triathlon at age 13 and, at age 16, become a professional triathlete. The cycling part of the triathlon became his focus, and he devoted his life to professional cycling. In that sport he has excelled as national and world champion, as Olympian, and as record-tying five-time winner of the Tour de France. He also started the Lance Armstrong Foundation. He is surely one of the all-time great cyclists.

Question 2: Does the above paragraph have unity?

Answer: No. The sentence *He also started the Lance Armstrong Foundation* does not deal with the same topic as that in the rest of the paragraph. The paragraph speaks about Lance Armstrong's athletic accomplishments. This sentence spoils the unity of the paragraph and should be removed.

EXERCISE 1. Some of the following paragraphs have unity; some do not. Read each paragraph carefully and tell which sentences, if any, are off the topic.

Sample 1:

[1]When Benjamin Franklin was a teenager, rivers were not so polluted as they are now. [2]For example, the day he arrived in Philadelphia in 1723, he went down to the wharf for a drink from the river. [3]Who would dare to drink water straight from a river today?

SENTENCES OFF THE TOPIC, IF ANY: *None*

(All the sentences deal with one topic: *river pollution.*)

Sample 2:

[1]Amelia Earhart had a brief but remarkable career in aviation. [2]In 1932 she became the first woman to fly alone across the Atlantic. [3]Three years later, she flew from Hawaii to California by herself. [4]No one had ever done this before. [5]In 1937, with copilot Frederick J. Noonan, she tried to fly around the world, but her plane disappeared in the middle of the Pacific, and no trace of it—or her—was ever found. [6]Amelia's first career was teaching. [7]Later, she became a writer. [8]In fact, at the time of her disappearance, she was married to George P. Putnam, a publisher.

SENTENCES OFF THE TOPIC, IF ANY: *Sentences 6, 7, and 8*

(The topic is *Amelia Earhart's aviation career.* Sentences 6, 7, and 8 do not deal with that topic.)

Paragraph 1

[1]A part-time job has many advantages. [2]First of all, it gives you money to spend on things you need or like, so that you don't have to keep asking for a bigger allowance. [3]Also, if you are thrifty, it enables you to save for the future, especially for college. [4]But most of all, it gives you a chance to contribute something to the family's expenses if your parents need the money. [5]They are sure to appreciate this help, and you will feel more responsible and independent.

SENTENCES OFF THE TOPIC, IF ANY: _____

Paragraph 2

[1]What do we mean by "global warming" and what causes it? [2]The surface temperature of the earth has risen by about 1 degree Fahrenheit over the past century. [3]The term means the warming of earth's atmosphere believed to be caused by accumulation of greenhouse gases. [4]The greenhouse gases mainly are carbon dioxide, methane, and nitrous oxide. [5]Nitrous oxide is sometimes called "laughing gas" and is used by dentists. [6]Many scientists believe that human activities, such as forest burning, use of fossil fuels, and nuclear fission, contribute to global warming.

SENTENCES OFF THE TOPIC, IF ANY: _____

Paragraph 3

   [1]Blue whales, the largest animals in the world, are in danger of being wiped out. [2]Because of their size, they have yielded the highest profits to the whaling industry, and they have been overhunted. [3]In the past, these gentle animals had a fighting chance because they had to be harpooned by hand from small boats at close range. [4]But in our century, they have been hunted with helicopters, sonar, and exploding harpoons fired from guns. [5]As a result, there may soon be no more blue whales in our oceans if their endangered status is not respected and laws against illegal hunting are not enforced. [6]*Moby Dick* is a novel about a huge white whale by Herman Melville.

SENTENCES OFF THE TOPIC, IF ANY: _____

If a paragraph has unity, then, it deals with one subject. There is another aspect of unity, however. All the sentences tell about one topic, but the sentences must also give unity by fitting together as a whole, that is, by relating to one another in a clear, logical way.

Read the following paragraph:

   Ms. O'Reilly offered three reasons why students should prepare well for class. Preparing for class helps develop self-discipline. Self-discipline is valuable. It promotes focus and organization. Preparing for class teaches responsibility. Responsibility means fulfillment of obligation, and that is part of being a good student. Preparing for class boosts learning. It reinforces what is being taught in the classroom. Ms. O'Reilly says that students who prepare well will benefit in three ways.

Is this a good paragraph? No, it really could be much better. All of the sentences talk about good class preparation and its benefits, but the sentences themselves seem choppy and somewhat unrelated.

Now read the revised paragraph:

   Ms. O'Reilly offered three reasons why students should prepare well for class. First, good class preparation helps develop self-discipline, which is a valuable quality, promoting focus and organization. Second, good preparation teaches responsibility because it means fulfillment of obligation, and that is part of being a successful student. Finally, preparation boosts learning by reinforcing what is being taught in the classroom. According to Ms. O'Reilly, therefore, students who prepare well will benefit in these three ways.

This paragraph is much better because the sentences are connected to each other. The words "First," "Second," and "Finally" organize the paragraph by clearly setting off the three reasons, and they act as transitions by linking one to the next. The addition of "therefore" to the final sentence unifies the entire paragraph by referring back to Ms. O'Reilly and her three reasons. Other words commonly used for transition include *however, furthermore, moreover, nonetheless,* and the like.

UNITY IN THE PARAGRAPH   **237**

The changes in sentence structure also promote unity in the paragraph. For example, in the original version, three sentences were devoted to the first reason, self-discipline. In the revised version, the three sentences become one sentence with interrelated parts.

EXERCISE 2.   Using transitions and variety in sentence structure, revise the following paragraph to give it greater unity.

So you would like to teach your dog some tricks? Three factors (besides the dog) are necessary. You must know about the personality and breed traits of your dog. Some dogs, such as terriers, are acrobatic. You must know the basics of giving opening commands and closing commands. The closing command is also called a release. You must also give time to the training. Each session should last only about five minutes. During the session, your attention should be focused on the dog. Not all dogs learn at the same rate, so another factor is patience accompanied by a calm, kind attitude. Sometimes the dog will not "get it." Reward him with a toy or a treat after every session. Always remember that an old dog can learn new tricks.

_____

_____

_____

_____

_____

_____

_____

_____

_____

_____

_____

Lesson 30 The Topic Sentence

 A *topic sentence* states the topic, or main idea, of a paragraph. It is usually the first sentence in its paragraph.

Here are some of the topic sentences we have already met:

What do we mean by "global warming" and what causes it?

A part-time job has many advantages.

Amelia Earhart had a brief but remarkable career in aviation.

Question: Why are topic sentences useful?

Answer: Topic sentences help us read and write better.

When we read, the topic sentence tells us what the paragraph will be about.

When we write, if we keep referring back to our topic sentence, it will keep us from going off the topic.

Not all paragraphs begin with a topic sentence. In fact, many paragraphs do not even have a topic sentence. Here, however, we are going to practice writing topic sentences because it is a good way to develop skill in composition.

EXERCISE.   Write a paragraph beginning with one of the topic sentences listed below. You may use a topic sentence of your own if you wish.

Suggested Topic Sentences
1. Some people just do not return things that they borrow.
2. I enjoy (*or* do not enjoy) being the oldest (*or* youngest, *or* only) child in the family.
3. Basketball (*or* some other sport) is an exciting sport to watch.
4. Dogs sometimes surprise us by their cleverness.
5. I like (*or* do not like) my neighborhood.

6. We waste a good part of our lives standing in lines.

7. The job of a police officer (*or* nurse) is not an easy one.

8. One of the best programs on television is _____.

9. The _____ team has had a good (*or* poor) season.

10. Saturday afternoon (*or* some other time) is the worst (*or* best) time to shop.

Your paragraph should consist of at least six or seven sentences. A model paragraph follows to show what you should do.

Model Paragraph

[1]Saturday afternoon is the worst time to shop. [2]It is the time when thousands of people rush to do their shopping for the week. [3]That explains why traffic is heavy on Saturday afternoon. [4]When you finally get to the stores, the aisles are crowded but the selection is poor. [5]Some of the items on your shopping list may not be available because they have been sold out. [6]Worst of all, the lines at the checkout counters are long and slow-moving. [7]By the time you get home, you will be tired and irritable, and you will probably have a headache.

Comments: The model paragraph consists of seven sentences. The topic sentence (S1) states that *Saturday afternoon is the worst time to shop*. All the other sentences support this statement.

S2 and S3 show how hard it is to get to the stores on Saturday afternoon.

S4, S5, and S6 describe the difficult conditions in stores on Saturday afternoon.

S7 deals with the effect of Saturday shopping on the shopper's nerves and health.

Note that the paragraph has unity because it deals with one topic, and every sentence in the paragraph stays on the topic.

Now write your paragraph.

_____

_____

_____

_____

_____

_____

_____

_____

_____

_____

_____

_____

_____

_____

_____

_____

Lesson 31 The Clincher Sentence

 A *clincher sentence* drives home the point that the paragraph is making.

Not all paragraphs have a clincher sentence. When there is one, it is the last sentence in the paragraph.

A good clincher sentence restates the main idea already mentioned in the topic sentence, but it does so more strongly, with the help of material brought out in the paragraph. *A clincher sentence should not merely repeat the topic sentence.*

The following paragraph is complete, except for the clincher sentence. What would be a good clincher sentence to end this paragraph?

[1]We waste a good part of our lives standing in lines. [2]In the morning, we stand in line to get a bus. [3]At noon, we stand in cafeteria lines. [4]In the library, we stand in line to borrow or return a book. [5]At the supermarket, we stand in checkout lines. [6]In the post office, we stand in line to mail a package, and in the bank we stand in line to wait for the teller to help us. [7]Even when we go to the movies to enjoy ourselves, we must often wait in long lines, and we are glad when we get in so we can finally sit down. [8]Sometimes we have to stand in line just to use a public restroom.

Questions: Which of the following would be weak clincher sentences for the above paragraph? Which would be good clincher sentences? Why?

CHOICE 1. All of us waste a good part of our lives standing in line.

CHOICE 2. Think how much more time we could have for the important things in life if we did not have to stand in line.

CHOICE 3. Wouldn't you agree that we waste a good part of our lives waiting in line?

CHOICE 4. What a waste of time and energy!

Answers: Choices 1 and 3 are weak. Choice 1 merely repeats the topic sentence.

Choice 3 is a little better. At least it turns the topic sentence into a question, and it involves the reader. But it is essentially the same as the topic sentence.

Choices 2 and 4 are better. Choice 2 builds on the hints in the paragraph that the things for which we stand in line are not too important, and it suggests that there are better uses for the time wasted standing in line.

Choice 4, building on a hint in S7, stresses the human energy, as well as the time, we waste by standing in line.

EXERCISE 1.   Write a suitable clincher sentence for the following paragraph. Be prepared to explain why your clincher sentence is a good one.

I do not enjoy being the oldest child in the family. If there is a fight or a quarrel, my brother and especially my sister are bound to get sympathy because they are younger. I am often unfairly blamed because, as I am told, I am "older and expected to know better." If either of them gets hurt when I am around, my mother is likely to say, "Why didn't you watch her?" or "Why didn't you watch him?" When my friends come over, my brother and sister sometimes annoy us by trying to get attention. When I try to do my homework, it is sometimes hard for me to concentrate because they keep the TV on too loud, watching some worthless program.

CLINCHER SENTENCE: _____

_____

_____

EXERCISE 2.   Write a suitable clincher sentence for the following paragraph. Again, be prepared to defend it.

Some people just do not return things that they borrow. Of course, I do not care about little, unimportant borrowings. For example, people often ask, "May I borrow a sheet of paper?" or "May I borrow a paper clip?" What they really mean is "Will you *give* me a sheet of paper or a paper clip?" They have no intention of giving it back, and I really do not expect them to. The same is true of pencils. How often has a teacher asked, "Will you lend so-and-so a pencil?" and how rarely has the thing been returned! But other things are more important. Once I lent someone my history notes when I needed them myself to study for a test. After two weeks, I practically had to beg the person to return them to me.

CLINCHER SENTENCE: _____

_____

_____

Lesson 32 Developing a Paragraph with Reasons

The previous lessons in Part Four have emphasized how a paragraph must have unity. It is not always so easy, however, to achieve that unity. Fortunately, there are a couple of practical methods that can help. In this lesson, we look at one of these methods, the use of reasons, as a way to develop paragraphs.

For example, you have just written this topic sentence:

One improvement that our community needs is better bus service.

You are trying to develop this topic sentence into a paragraph, but you cannot write another word. You sit and stare at your paper or computer screen.

Has this ever happened to you? If so, it will be less likely to happen again—once you have learned the method of **giving reasons.**

The following paragraph shows how to develop a topic sentence by giving reasons.

Model Paragraph

[1]One improvement that our community needs is better bus service. [2]At present, all we have are four old buses running between the railroad station and the community park. [3]These buses are very crowded, and they are rarely on time. [4]After 8 P.M. there is no bus service at all, even though a number of shops and the library are open until 9. [5]Recently, because gasoline costs have remained high, more people have been riding the buses, and the overcrowding is worse than ever. [6]The aging buses are being strained to the limit. [7]Breakdowns are becoming more frequent. [8]Unless new buses are put into service soon, we are going to have a real transportation crisis in this town.

Comments on the Model Paragraph

S1 (the topic sentence) states: *One improvement that our community needs is better bus service.*

S2–S7 (the body of the paragraph) support this statement with *reasons:*

old buses (S2)
crowding and lateness (S3)
lack of service after 8 P.M. (S4)
recent increases in ridership and overcrowding (S5)

overtaxing of the buses (S6)
breakdowns (S7)

S8 (the clincher sentence) sums up the paragraph and restates the idea of the topic sentence with greater emphasis.

Arranging the Reasons

The following paragraph is the same as the one you have just read, except that some of the reasons appear in a different order.

Question: Is the following paragraph better than the one we have just read? Why?

[1]One improvement that our community needs is better bus service. [2]At present, all we have are four old buses running between the railroad station and the community park. [3]These buses are very crowded, and they are rarely on time. [4]Recently, because of the high cost of gasoline, more people have been riding the buses, and the overcrowding is worse than ever. [5]The aging buses are being strained to the limit. [6]Breakdowns are becoming more frequent. [7]After 8 P.M. there is no bus service at all, even though a number of shops and the library are open until 9. [8]Unless new buses are put into service soon, we are going to have a real transportation crisis in this town.

Answer: The above paragraph is not as good as the first one because it presents its reasons in the following order:

> old buses (S2)
> crowding and lateness (S3)
> recent increases in ridership and overcrowding (S4)
> overtaxing of the buses (S5)
> breakdowns (S6)
> lack of service after 8 P.M. (S7)

This is not the most effective order.

The most compelling reasons are the *recent increases in ridership, overtaxing of the buses, and, most important of all, breakdowns.* In the original paragraph these reasons are given *just before the clincher sentence.*

But what do we find in the important position just before the clincher sentence in the second version of the paragraph? We find a much weaker reason—*lack of service after 8 P.M.*

Hints for Arranging Reasons

1. Begin with a strong reason, but not your strongest. Example:

   At present, all we have are four old buses . . .

2. End the paragraph with your strongest reason, or put it just before the clincher sentence if there is one. Example:

   Breakdowns are becoming more frequent.

EXERCISE 1.   Each of the following topic sentences can be developed into a paragraph with **reasons.** Three reasons are given. Which should you mention first? Last? Put an **F** in the space before your first reason and an **L** before your last. Be prepared to defend your answers.

Sample:

TOPIC SENTENCE: **Our mayor deserves to be reelected.**

_____ 1. He has speeded up street repairs.

___L___ 2. He has helped the city achieve the highest level of employment in the state.

___F___ 3. He has eliminated wasteful spending and government inefficiency.

1. TOPIC SENTENCE: **TV news programs are worth watching.**

   _____ 1. You can see and hear the people in the news.

   _____ 2. You get weather reports.

   _____ 3. You get up-to-the-minute news.

2. TOPIC SENTENCE: **Benjamin Franklin was a remarkable person.**

   _____ 1. He invented the lightning rod.

   _____ 2. He persuaded France to come to our aid, enabling us to win our independence.

   _____ 3. He was the finest American writer of his time, as well as a practical scientist.

3. TOPIC SENTENCE: **The fire at Ace Supermarket has hurt the people of our neighborhood.**

   _____ 1. Since Ace burned down, shoppers have been paying more elsewhere but not getting the same quality.

   _____ 2. Ace used to offer the best merchandise at the lowest prices.

   _____ 3. Ace's dairy and meat products were of the highest quality.

4. TOPIC SENTENCE: **I have decided to give up my paper route.**

_____1. I am pressed for time now that I am on the basketball team.

_____ 2. Some of my customers are slow in paying.

_____ 3. Delivering newspapers is not as much fun as it used to be.

5. TOPIC SENTENCE: **The disadvantages of motor vehicles are serious.**

_____ 1. They are a major cause of air pollution, endangering the nation's health.

_____ 2. They destroy billions of dollars of property annually.

_____ 3. They kill thousands of people (43,000 in 2002) a year on our roads and highways.

Now you should try writing your own paragraph with *reasons.* Choose one of the following topic sentences and develop it. If you wish, you may use a topic sentence of your own.

Suggestion: Jot down your reasons and arrange them in the most effective order before writing your paragraph.

A model paragraph follows, together with explanatory comments, to help you write your own paragraph in Exercise 2.

Suggested Topic Sentences

1. Our community needs a new athletic field (*or* more parking facilities, *or some other improvement*).
2. The computer (*or* the airplane, the automobile, television, *etc.*) is one of the miracles of modern living.
3. Unemployment is a serious problem.
4. Spring (*or* summer, fall, *or* winter) is the season I enjoy most.
5. A calculator is useful to own.
6. The death penalty should (*or* should not) be abolished.
7. Smoking is harmful to your health.
8. It is (*or* is not yet) time that we elected a woman to be our country's president.

Model Paragraph

¹Fall is the season I enjoy most. ²It is a pleasure to be outdoors in the fall because there are few mosquitoes and the weather is mild. ³The colorful autumn leaves make the outdoors more beautiful. ⁴When I finish classes on a fall day, I can't wait to get out on the hockey field or just take my time walking home with friends. ⁵I always feel better and have more energy in the fall than in any other season. ⁶If it were up to me, I would have nothing but fall all year round.

Comments on the Model Paragraph

S1 (the topic sentence) states: *Fall is the season I enjoy most.*

S2–S5 (the body of the paragraph) support that statement with *reasons*:

> pleasure to be outdoors; few mosquitoes; mild weather (S2)
> colorful leaves (S3)
> fine time for playing hockey and walking (S4)
> season when I feel best and most energetic (S5)

S6 (the clincher sentence) repeats the thought of the topic sentence in different words and with greater emphasis.

Arranging the Reasons—Another Look

Note the order of the reasons given to support the topic sentence. The first reason offered is a strong one—but not the strongest:

> It is a pleasure to be outdoors . . . (S2)

The strongest reason is given last—just before the clincher sentence:

> I always feel better and have more energy in the fall . . . (S5)

In fact, S5 is so strong that if the clincher sentence (S6) were omitted, we would still have an effective paragraph.

EXERCISE 2.   Write your own paragraph.

_____

_____

_____

_____

_____

_____

_____

_____

_____

_____

_____

_____

_____

_____

_____

_____

Lesson 33 Developing a Paragraph with Examples

Lesson 32 showed how reasons can be used to develop a unified paragraph. Another method is the use of **examples.** Examples add interest to your writing and support your ideas. They help to explain a topic by putting a "face" to the "name" of things.

Consider the following. Suppose a speaker is describing the Bill of Rights. We listen, but we do not really understand. Seeing that we are confused, the speaker says, "Let me give you an example of what the Bill of Rights means. If there were no Bill of Rights, you could be thrown into prison without being informed of the charges against you. And you could be kept there for the rest of your life without being brought to trial."

Thanks to the example, we begin to understand the protection that the Bill of Rights gives us.

Examples, then, are valuable in explaining. The following paragraph shows how to develop a topic sentence by giving examples:

Model Paragraph

^{1}Often, we see a lack of respect for the law. ^{2}There are laws against dumping in this town, but they are not being obeyed. ^{3}Go to any vacant lot and look around. ^{4}Under the "no dumping" signs you will find old tires, rusting sinks, junked refrigerators, and other trash. ^{5}There are also laws about the care of dogs, but some dog-owners seem to be ignorant of them. ^{6}They let their dogs run loose and do not clean up after them. ^{7}It is against the law to put out garbage in open containers, yet we find uncovered garbage cans almost everywhere. ^{8}Animals get into these cans and knock them over, creating an unsightly and unsanitary mess. ^{9}Perhaps the most disregarded of all laws are our traffic regulations. ^{10}More and more drivers are speeding, going through red lights, and double parking. ^{11}And some drivers, apparently not even worrying about being fined, have been parking in spaces clearly marked as reserved for the disabled.

Comments on the Model Paragraph

S1 (the topic sentence) indicates that there is *a lack of respect for the law.*

The rest of the paragraph explains that lack of respect by means of *examples:*

dumping violations (S2–S4)
dog-care violations (S5–S6)
garbage violations (S7–S8)
traffic violations (S9–S11)

Question 1:   Why are the violations of the traffic laws discussed last?

Answer: They are the *most disregarded of all laws*. The breaking of these laws furnishes the writer with the strongest examples of *a lack of respect for the law*.

Remember that the end of the paragraph is the all-important place for making the final impression on the reader. It is a good place for your strongest material. As with reasons, example can be arranged in order of increasing importance, though sometimes there is no clear order (see, for example, Number 3 of Exercise 1).

Question 2:   Why is there no clincher sentence?

Answer: None is needed. The examples in the paragraph all make the point that there is *a lack of respect for the law*. The last sentence (S11) is as emphatic as any clincher sentence can be.

EXERCISE 1.   Each topic sentence below can be developed into a paragraph by *examples*. Two examples are mentioned. Add a third.

Sample:

TOPIC SENTENCE: **Dogs do many wonderful things for their owners.**

Examples:
1. They give love.
2. They provide companionship.
3. *They protect property.*

1. TOPIC SENTENCE: **A power failure causes serious problems.**

Examples:
1. The lights go out.
2. Refrigerators stop working.
3. _____

2. TOPIC SENTENCE: **There are several ways to cheer up a sick friend.**

Examples:
1. You can send the friend a "get-well" card.
2. You can telephone the friend.
3. _____

3. TOPIC SENTENCE: **Shoppers pay for merchandise in different ways.**

   Examples:

   1. Some use a credit card.

   2. Some write a check.

   3. _____

4. TOPIC SENTENCE: **Each of us can do something to save energy.**

   Examples:

   1. We can walk on short errands instead of going by car.

   2. We can turn off the lights when a room is not in use.

   3. _____

5. TOPIC SENTENCE: **Yesterday's snowstorm paralyzed a large section of our state.**

   Examples:

   1. Most airports had to shut down.

   2. Many people could not get to work.

   3. _____

EXERCISE 2. Choose one of the following topic sentences and develop it into a paragraph by giving *examples.* You may use a topic sentence of your own, if you wish. A sample paragraph follows.

Suggested Topic Sentences

1. Americans are fond of foreign cars (*or* ethnic foods).

2. Television has some very entertaining (*or* boring) commercials.

3. There are several ways to prepare for a test.

4. Some people are not happy with their jobs.

5. Every member of my family helps with the household work.

6. There is room for improvement in the way our student government is run.

7. Our community park has much to offer.

8. Electricity does much of the work in our homes.

Model Paragraph

   [1]Americans are fond of ethnic foods. [2]Often, they go to Chinese restaurants for moo goo gai pan or shrimp lo mein. [3]When they visit a bakery, they are quite likely to buy Danish pastry, French eclairs, or Jewish rye bread. [4]On St. Patrick's Day and at other times, they enjoy corned beef and cabbage without necessarily being Irish. [5]They are especially fond of

Italian foods. [6]What American has not had spaghetti and meatballs, or macaroni and cheese, or pizza?

Comments:

S1 (the topic sentence) states: *Americans are fond of ethnic foods.*

S2–S6 (the rest of the paragraph) support that statement with *examples:*

Chinese food (S2)
Danish, French, and Jewish food (S3)
Irish food (S4)
Italian food (S5 and S6)

Note that Italian food, the writer's strongest example, is discussed last.

Write your own paragraph.

_____

_____

_____

_____

_____

_____

_____

_____

_____

_____

_____

_____

_____

_____

_____

_____

_____

_____

Lesson 34 Varying Sentence Beginnings

Most English sentences begin with the subject.

> ***Traffic*** is usually heavy in the morning.
> SUBJ.

In Lesson 19 (page 133), we learned that sentences do not always need to start with the subject—nor should they. Sometimes there are good reasons for not beginning with the subject. Here are two:

Reason 1: To emphasize something other than the subject.

Suppose, for example, that you wish to emphasize the TIME when traffic is usually heavy. In that case, you may begin with the prepositional phrase *in the morning*.

> ***In the morning,*** traffic is usually heavy.
> PREP. PHR.

Or suppose you want to emphasize that it is USUAL for traffic to be heavy in the morning. In that case, you may begin with the adverb *usually*.

> ***Usually*** traffic is heavy in the morning.
> ADV.

Reason 2: To hold the reader's interest.

Think how boring it would be for the reader if sentence after sentence were to begin in the same way—with the subject. Note how Thomas Hardy, in the following passage from *Tess of the D'Urbervilles,* makes his writing more interesting by varying his sentence beginnings:

> [1]He heard something behind him, the brush of feet. [2]Turning, he saw over the prostrate columns another figure; then, before he was aware, another was at hand on the right, under a trilithon, and another on the left. [3]The dawn shone full on the front of the man westward, and Clare could discern from this that he was tall and walked as if trained. [4]They all closed in with evident purpose. [5]Her story, then, was true! [6]Springing to his feet, he looked around for a weapon, loose stone, means of escape, anything. [7]By this time the nearest man was upon him.

How Thomas Hardy Begins His Sentences:

S1. *He* (subject)

S2. *Turning* (participle)

S3. *The dawn* (subject)

S4. *They* (subject)

S5. *Her story* (subject)

S6. *Springing to his feet* (participial phrase)

S7. *By this time* (prepositional phrase)

Question: What does Thomas Hardy gain by beginning S2 with the participle *Turning,* S6 with the participial phrase *Springing to his feet,* and S7 with the prepositional phrase *By this time?*

Answers: 1. He is able to emphasize the ideas expressed by the participle *Turning,* the participial phrase *Springing to her feet,* and the prepositional phrase *By this time.* Evidently he considers these ideas important to the sense and impact of the paragraph.

2. He is able to vary his sentence beginnings, making his writing more interesting.

Cautions: 1. Do not use a non-subject beginning, such as an adverb or a prepositional phrase, unless it expresses an idea you wish to emphasize.

2. Do not overuse non-subject beginnings. Most of your sentences should begin with the subject because that is the nature of English.

The following exercises give you practice in beginning sentences with *adverbs* and *prepositional phrases.* There are, of course, still other ways to begin sentences; see Lesson 19, page 133, for different ways to achieve variety.

EXERCISE 1. Rewrite each sentence twice. On **line *a*** begin with an *adverb.* On **line *b*** begin with a *prepositional phrase.*

Sample:

The lights were already on inside the ballpark.

a. Already the lights were on inside the ballpark.

b. Inside the ballpark the lights were already on.

1. I would certainly feel lost without my contact lenses.

a. _____

b. _____

2. Lange was evidently dissatisfied from the start.

   a. _____

   b. _____

3. You can get a bargain in a sale occasionally.

   a. _____

   b. _____

4. A crowd soon gathered outside the store.

   a. _____

   b. _____

5. We met your cousin at the beach recently.

   a. _____

   b. _____

6. You will undoubtedly improve with more experience.

   a. _____

   b. _____

7. Ramon once saw a deer near the pond.

   a. _____

   b. _____

8. The star was injured on the play, unfortunately.

   a. _____

   b. _____

9. A foreign language is sometimes bewildering to a beginner.

   a. _____

   _____

   b. _____

   _____

10. The chemistry student repeatedly got the same results in several runs of the experiment.

   a. _____

   _____

   b. _____

   _____

Read the following passage:

¹M. Madeleine is the mayor of a small French town. ²He is a fine public servant. ³He is, surprisingly, a newcomer to the town. ⁴He has been living there about seven years. ⁵The town at his arrival was in bad condition. ⁶Many of the inhabitants were out of work. ⁷Some families, in fact, were at the brink of starvation. ⁸M. Madeleine invented a process for manufacturing goods more cheaply. ⁹He opened a factory. ¹⁰He created many worthwhile jobs. ¹¹He brought back good times. ¹²The people now call him Father Madeleine. ¹³They love and respect him. ¹⁴They do not, however, know his real name. ¹⁵He is Jean-Valjean, an ex-convict. ¹⁶The police have been looking for him for years.

You may have recognized this story line—it describes part of the plot of *Les Miserables* by Victor Hugo. You may also have noticed, as you were reading the above passage, that **every sentence begins with the subject.** If some of the sentences were to begin with an *adverb* or a *prepositional phrase,* the passage would be greatly improved.

EXERCISE 2.   Rewrite *five* of the sentences in the above passage. In each case make the sentence begin with an *adverb* or a *prepositional phrase,* instead of the subject. Indicate the number of each sentence you write.

Sample:

SENTENCE NO. ___3___   *Surprisingly, he is a newcomer to the town.*

1. SENTENCE NO. _____

2. SENTENCE NO. _____

3. SENTENCE NO. _____

4. SENTENCE NO. _____

5. SENTENCE NO. _____

EXERCISE 3. Now try your hand at creating a paragraph with both unity and variety. Write a paragraph of at least seven sentences, giving some information about a person, animal, place, or thing. You may write on one of the topics suggested below, or on a topic of your own.

Suggested Topics

1. A member of your family
2. A friend or a classmate
3. A beach, lake, or park
4. A neighborhood shop or restaurant
5. Your city, town, or community
6. A cat, dog, or other pet
7. Your school
8. The family car

Hints: In your first sentence, identify the person, animal, place, or thing you are writing about.

In the rest of the paragraph, give details that will help the reader understand your topic.

Important: Begin at least one sentence with an adverb and one with a prepositional phrase.

A sample composition follows.

Model Composition
"A Classmate"

^{1}Marie is one of our new classmates. ^{2}She recently arrived from Haiti. ^{3}At first she had a hard time because she spoke only French. ^{4}She has a warm smile and a friendly personality. ^{5}Everyone likes her. ^{6}Already she has made several friends. ^{7}They are helping her learn English.

Comments

S1 identifies Marie as *one of our new classmates.*

The rest of the paragraph gives further details about Marie:

    her home country (S2)
    her language problem (S3)
    her personality (S4 and S5)
    the friends she has made and the help they are giving her (S6 and S7)

Note that S3 begins with the prepositional phrase *At first,* and S6 with the adverb *Already.*

Write your paragraph.

_____
_____
_____
_____
_____
_____
_____
_____
_____
_____
_____
_____
_____
_____
_____

Index